ten minute
stress
relief

ten minute
stress
relief

ERICA BREALEY

Bounty
Books

First published in the United Kingdom in 2002 by Cassell & Co,

This edition published 2006 by Bounty Books,
a division of Octopus Publishing Group Ltd,
2-4 Heron Quays, London E14 4JP.

A CIP catalogue record for this book is available from the British Library

ISBN-13: 978-0-753707-36-4
ISBN-10: 0-753707-36-5
Jacket design by Justin Hunt
Special photography by Paul Bricknell
Author photograph by Robin Farquhar Thomson

Shri Yantra (p. 124) © Ajit Mookerjee Collection/courtesy
Thames & Hudson Ltd, London
Images on pp. 9, 19, 26, 29, 33, 35, 40, 77, 79, 98, 101, 104 and 112 © Corbis

Printed and bound in Toppan Printing Company In China.

**If you are pregnant or if you have a medical condition
that could be adversely affected by exercise or any doubts
about your health, consult a doctor before embarking on
any exercise programme.**

contents

introduction

'The time to relax is when you don't have any time for it.'
Sydney Harris

When you're stressed to the max – crises at work, impossible deadlines, kids off the rails, relationships in tatters – finding the time to relax can just pile on the pressure. But the truth is that no one is too busy to snatch the odd ten minutes for themselves, and the busier you are the greater you need for time to switch off, relax and recharge.

Relieving stress does not have to mean long sessions sweating it out in the gym or spending hours on end in steam baths complete with seaweed wraps. If you do not have the luxury of time, complicated workouts and lengthy treatments are not for you. But this does not mean you are doomed to suffer the ill-effects of stress. The good news is that stress can be effectively relieved in very little time at all.

Just a few minutes devoted to effective relaxation can not only reverse the damaging effects of unrelieved stress, which can wreak havoc with your health as well as undermining career, relationships and well-being – but can also make stress work for you in positive ways. Under your control, stress can become a potent source of energy, creativity and enjoyment in your life.

We often forget that stress is a perfectly normal response to a challenge or threat, releasing a cocktail of hormones within the body which instantly put you on the alert and enable you to rise to the occasion and take appropriate action. It is only when stress is prolonged, and stress hormones continue to bombard your body, that it becomes hazardous to your health and psyche. Few of us like to admit that we're finding it difficult to cope, but recognizing that you are under too much stress is an important first step towards handling it.

There are two broad approaches to dealing with stress. The first focuses on its causes, and involves thinking through problems, coming up with alternatives, and taking appropriate action. Not all problems can be easily resolved, however, which brings us to the second approach. This concentrates on people, not problems, and involves practical ways to relax and relieve stress, whatever its cause. This book is mainly concerned with the second approach to stress.

How to **use this book**

When time is at a premium, the art of stress relief is to use fast and effective relaxation techniques that really work, enabling you to switch off whenever you choose from stressful situations. *Ten-Minute Stress Relief* gives you tried and tested procedures and strategies that have been found to achieve maximum relaxation in minimum time. All the procedures described in the book can be carried out in ten minutes, while others require little or no time at all – more a shift in awareness.

Ten-Minute Stress Relief takes a holistic approach, integrating mental and physical relaxation techniques, to alleviate and control stress of all kinds and for all personalities. Part 1 explains the basics of stress, Part 2 the principles of holistic stress relief, and Part 3 describes ten-minute routines for achieving a quiet mind and a relaxed body, quick-fix stress-busting techniques and strategies for emergency situations, and gives you golden rules for keeping calm, whatever the pressures.

To achieve maximum stress reduction – as well as maximum physical and psychological benefits – practise a balanced combination of techniques for mental, physical and spiritual relaxation, taking one step at a time. If you overdo it, you are less likely to keep it up. Begin with the technique or techniques that seem most appropriate or appealing, and practise for a week or so, then take stock. Over time experiment further and build up your own repertoire, combining practices in whatever way works best for you.

Ten minutes a day or, even better, two or three ten-minute blocks devoted to relaxation techniques can not only relieve stress but make a dramatic difference to your overall health and quality of life. The more you practise the easier it becomes, and the better you feel.

Good luck!

understanding

stress

what is **stress?**

Stress is the body's physiological response to pressure, especially to events that seem threatening, challenging or involve change. Ever-increasing working hours and the sheer pace of life and change have sent our stress levels soaring, creating an epidemic of stress-related illnesses. Stress now accounts for more time taken off work than minor complaints such as the common cold. And like the common cold, stress is infectious, as anyone who lives or works closely with a carrier can tell you.

Because it gets a bad press, it is easy to forget that stress can be positive as well as negative. Too little stress means there is little challenge in your life, and can be a sign that you lack purpose or that you are not making the most of your personal skills and talents. By contrast moderate doses of short-term stress not only boost the immune system and help you to fight off infection, but also mobilize your mental resources, so that you think more creatively, get more done and perform better.

stress is infectious, as anyone who lives or works closely with a carrier can tell you

When the number of demands made on you exceeds your ability to cope, however, you are under too much stress. If this persists and stress becomes chronic, you are at risk of mental or physical breakdown.

Stress that goes on and on, unabated, raises hormone levels in the body for prolonged periods, compromising the immune system and placing enormous strain on the cardiovascular system. The litany of stress-related diseases is long and probably familiar.

Research shows that people under a lot of stress at work are twice as likely to develop coronary heart disease. As well as heart attacks, chronic stress causes hypertension, migraine and insomnia, and plays a role in many other diseases such as cancer, arthritis and respiratory disorders. Stress is also associated with emotional and psychological problems such as anxiety, panic attacks, lack of concentration, loss of memory and depression. Parental stress damages children and even babies still in the womb. Good reason, if any, to put into regular practice stress-relieving techniques that allow body and mind to recover their natural state of balance and dramatically reduce the risk of suffering any of the above illnesses.

The art of handling stress lies in recognizing when you have the right amount of stress in your life and in acquiring the ability to switch off from stressful situations so that you can relax and recover. Optimum stress levels maximize energy, enthusiasm and achievement, yet leave you feeling relaxed and open to new challenges.

Stress–performance curve

Not all stress is bad for you. A certain amount releases creativity, gives spice to life, and enhances performance. Finding the right balance for you, personally, is the key to achieving your potential and to personal fulfilment and growth.

Many people readily acknowledge that they work better under pressure, but performance improves with pressure only up to a certain point, after which it reaches a plateau and, if pressure persists, declines. If pressure continues unabated you may begin to experience early warning signals (see pp. 18–19) that you are overstretched. If you ignore exhaustion and other stress signals, you risk burning out and having a mental or physical breakdown.

The stress-performance curve below shows the normal reaction to stress, and how stress affects performance.

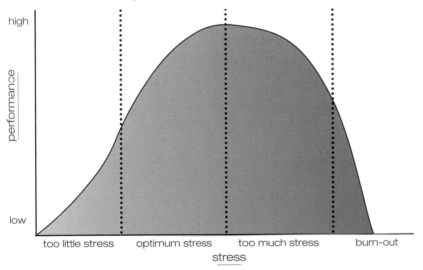

• Too little stress: insufficient challenge leads to boredom, low productivity and a lack of personal achievement; these in turn contribute to poor self-esteem and a feeling that there is little purpose to life.

• Optimum stress: the right amount of stress in your life enables you to take advantage of opportunities, rise to a challenge and expand your limits; you take problems in your stride and derive satisfaction from a job or jobs done well.

• Too much stress: despite physical or mental exhaustion, you drive yourself to keep going, but with diminishing returns; by constantly pushing yourself beyond your limits, you go into overdrive and find yourself unable to switch off and relax.

• Burn-out: the warning signals (see pp. 18–19) that you are under excessive stress are ringing loud and clear, and if you do not heed them you are liable to mental or physical breakdown; performance is erratic, at best.

fight or flight

People vary enormously in their perception of what is a stressful situation, but the physiological way our bodies respond to something we interpret as a threat – whether physical, mental or emotional, or simply challenging – is the same. Stress activates a part of the brain called the hypothalamus, setting off a complicated chain of biochemical events that causes a rush of adrenaline and noradrenaline into the system, rapidly followed by cortisol. Within a split second these hormones flood the body and circulate through the bloodstream, reaching all the organs and activating every cell in the body.

At this point our bodies start to work in a different way. The liver releases sugar and fatty acids into the bloodstream to boost energy. We breathe more rapidly, increasing the amount of oxygen in the body. Our hearts beat faster and our blood pressure rises, increasing the circulation of blood to the brain to enable quick thinking and swift decisions, and to the muscles to enable fast action. Our mouths go dry as blood is diverted away to the organs where it is most needed, and we start to sweat – the body's mechanism for cooling us down. We are now prepared for immediate action: to fight or, if we don't fancy our chances, to flee.

If the stress response, also known as the fight–flight response, is followed by physical activity, as it was designed to be, the energy released into the system by stress hormones is used up, allowing our bodies to relax and return to their normal state of balance.

This primitive stress response is common to all mammals when confronted with a potentially threatening situation or the sudden appearance of a predator. If a sleeping dog or cat is startled by a sudden noise, it jumps up, hackles raised, ready for action. In a split second it assesses the situation and prepares to fight or take flight or, if satisfied there is no threat, it settles down again and becomes calm. Either way, the stress hormones are metabolized.

What animals do not do is carry on thinking about alarming situations and problems once the immediate danger has passed, so the stress-inducing situations they encounter are interspersed with periods of recovery. Their outer calm is a reflection of their inner calm. We, with our well-developed psyches, are prone to go on and on thinking about anything that is worrying or upsetting us. This inability to switch off is what keeps our stress levels raised, resulting in prolonged or chronic stress.

The fight–flight response evolved over millions of years to deal with emergencies and was very well suited to early man, whose very survival depended on the ability to fight or to escape. It is still vital to our survival, but few of the stresses we are faced with today call for either fight or flight. If stress is prolonged, our bodies remain in a state of physiological arousal with an excess of the stress hormones adrenaline and cortisol.

It is this unspent energy that causes the damage.

what's your type?

Life events such as the death of someone you love, divorce, getting fired or financial crises are highly traumatic and stressful for virtually everyone, but the ways in which any two people respond to the same potentially stressful situation differ enormously. This is partly because the kinds of situations that stress people vary according to natural talent and past experience: some people thrive on deadlines while others loathe them, some get a kick out of public speaking while others come out in a rash at the very thought. It is not events themselves so much as the way we perceive them that causes us stress.

Some personalities, known as Type As, are much more susceptible to high levels of stress and the associated illnesses. The typical Type A is an impatient, competitive, aggressive individual who lives life at a frenetic pace and expects everyone else around them to be as driven as they are. Type A tends to operate in crisis mode most of the time and is always in a rush. He or she talks in a hurry, walks in a hurry, eats in a hurry and can't bear waiting for anything – not for a bus, nor even for people to finish what they are saying. If Type A thinks others are too slow to make a point he or she is likely to interrupt or finish their point for them. Type A avoids boring repetitive tasks whenever possible and cannot bear to sit and do nothing. Type A is easily irritated and highly critical of others, though often oversensitive to criticism directed towards him or herself. Type As have little patience with people less able than themselves, and find other people's mistakes hard to tolerate. In short, Type As generate much of their own stress.

Type B, by contrast, is pretty laid back. He or she has a philosophical approach to life, taking it as it comes, one thing at a time, without feeling any kind of time-urgency. He or she gets on with work in a calm relaxed way, though this does not necessarily imply a lack of ambition. However, there is more to life than work for Type B, who has plenty of other interests and hobbies. Type B is relaxed, self-assured and pleasant to be with.

Most people are somewhere between the two extremes, neither one nor the other, but predominantly Type A or Type B, or a healthy AB. Type A behaviour is becoming increasingly common, however, in our task-oriented culture of achievement, and this is leading to an increase in stress-related disease. Extreme Type As are at much greater risk of suffering a heart attack than Type Bs, and are also more prone to cancer, migraines and other disease.

The good news is that Type A behaviour can be modified. If you recognize yourself, at least in part, in the description of Type A above, or if you score above 50 in the following self-assessment test, then following the strategies and techniques described in this book will help you to alter destructive behaviour patterns and significantly improve your chances of living into a healthy old age.

15

self-assessment

The following pairs of statements represent extreme behaviour patterns at opposite ends of the Type A–Type B spectrum. Score your answers by choosing the most appropriate number from 1 to 7.

When waiting for an appointment or to be served in a restaurant, you sit back and relax.	1 2 3 4 5 6 7	Waiting makes you feel edgy and you are aggravated by any delay.
You play games and sports for the sheer fun of it. The result is less important than the play.	1 2 3 4 5 6 7	You always play to win – even against the kids.
You are a good listener and always wait for others to finish what they are saying.	1 2 3 4 5 6 7	You can't wait to have your say and often interrupt others or finish their words for them.
You are never hurried in your actions, even when the heat is on and you are under pressure.	1 2 3 4 5 6 7	You are always in a rush, anxious to be moving on to the next thing on your list.
You have plenty of interests and hobbies outside of work.	1 2 3 4 5 6 7	Work is of overriding importance, often dominating your free time.
You have a balanced social life, and maintain regular contact with a wide circle of friends and family.	1 2 3 4 5 6 7	Your social life revolves around work interests and colleagues.
You are satisfied with your job and content with your position at work.	1 2 3 4 5 6 7	You are highly ambitious, looking for rapid promotion and advancement of your career.
You are a careful and courteous driver, always making way for other vehicles and pedestrians.	1 2 3 4 5 6 7	You are an aggressive driver, impatient of others on the road and anxious to get ahead, even if it means taking risks.

Work brings its own reward through the fulfilment and satisfaction you derive from your job.

1 2 3 4 5 6 7 You crave recognition and praise for a job well done.

You eat slowly and enjoy each mouthful.

1 2 3 4 5 6 7 You eat quickly, often finishing your meal before others are barely half way through.

You respect people for who they are rather than what they are, and you never judge people by position, possessions or the size of their bank balance.

1 2 3 4 5 6 7 Your measure your own and other people's worth in terms of numbers: how many achievements, how much money, and so on.

You are in touch with your feelings and able to express them appropriately.

1 2 3 4 5 6 7 You suppress your feelings but betray them through angry outbursts, critical remarks or irritability.

17

Score 66–84: extreme type A

Highly competitive and always striving to be in control, you drive yourself hard. Because you are unaware how tense you really are, you do little to alleviate stress, but unless you moderate your behaviour you risk heart disease and other stress-related problems.

Score 48–65: moderate type A

Watch yourself and take care not to push yourself too hard. Be sure to take regular time out for yourself to unwind and relax.

Score 36–47: healthy type AB

You enjoy a challenge but have a well-balanced life and do not let pressure get the better of you. Be careful to ensure that Type A behaviour doesn't begin to dominate when opportunities open up or your ambitions expand.

Score 18–35: moderate Type B

You have a relaxed and healthy approach to life and are unlikely to suffer from stress-related illnesses.

Score 12–17: extreme type B

You are so laid back and easy-going that you hardly know what stress is. You are not at risk of stress-related problems.

warning signs

Stress has a habit of creeping up on us unawares. Even when the overload signals – tiredness and irritability, headaches, waking up at night with problems turning round and round – are flashing, we often ignore them or just pop a few pain-relieving pills in the hope that that will take care of that. But the problem with ignoring stress while it is still perfectly manageable is that it builds up until you reach breaking point. By learning to spot the signs of stress you can take steps to relieve it before it becomes a serious problem.

Early-warning signs
The first signs that things are getting on top of you and you are overstretched may be:
- irritability, impatience, being edgy and uptight, snapping at others, tending to blame them for the fact that you are in a bad mood
- oversensitivity, easily taking offence where none is intended, being liable to see things in a negative light
- feeling tired but being unable to sleep, or sleeping badly and waking up unrefreshed
- a change in your normal eating habits, eating either more or less, and often replacing meals and healthy snacks with fast food and chocolate
- relying more and more on alcohol, cigarettes or other drugs
- feeling sick, getting tummy upsets, diarrhoea or constipation
- nervous twitches and habits like nail-biting, scratching or knee-jiggling.

Mental symptoms of stress
- lack of concentration or attention, forgetfulness
- inability to think clearly, difficulty in making simple decisions
- loss of perspective, obsessing over details
- a nagging feeling of being under pressure of time
- mental exhaustion, burn-out.

Emotional symptoms of stress
- increased anxiety, panic attacks
- loss of self-esteem
- depression and negativity
- feelings of hostility and resentment
- moodiness, tearfulness
- lack of a sense of humour
- nightmares.

Physical symptoms of stress

- muscular tension and fatigue
- head, shoulder, neck and backaches
- tired eyes, muscle-twitching at the corners of the eyes
- dry mouth, stiff jaw
- sweaty palms, cold fingers
- indigestion, heartburn
- frequent urination, bladder infections
- breathlessness, erratic breathing, hyperventilation
- heart palpitations
- frequent colds and headaches
- weight loss or gain
- impotence, loss of libido.

Behavioural symptoms of stress

- angry outbursts and aggression
- non-stop talking, often interrupting others
- nervous habits such as nail-biting, hair-pulling, finger-tapping, knee-jiggling
- workaholism or absenteeism
- social withdrawal
- neglecting appearance or hygiene
- obsessive-compulsive behaviour, such as checking and rechecking that doors are locked, washing hands over and over.

19

by learning to recognize the signs of stress you can take steps to prevent it building up and out of control

part 2

surviving

stress

get your life

Sophisticated technology and instant global communications make it increasingly possible to work any time, and anywhere, and it is harder than ever to strike the right balance between work and our private lives. We have become a nation of workaholics, many of us working long hours to climb corporate ladders at the expense of partners, families, friendships and our health.

Even when cherished ambitions are achieved we often feel strangely unhappy and unfulfilled. Instead of sitting back and enjoying the fruits of our labours, we find ourselves stuck on a treadmill of unremitting

in balance

deadlines and targets. With our lives out of balance, we end up suffering acute stress, with all the associated risks of mental and physical breakdown.

If you do not want to lose out to stress, it is vital to get your life in balance. When the balance is right, with space for Life – relationships, interests, fun – as well as for work, you protect yourself not only against stress, but against the vicissitudes of life. A balanced life is as vital to your health and happiness as a balanced diet, and key to avoiding the damaging effects of stress. So, assess your life regularly and redress the balance if it is too far out.

body

Paradoxically, we often lose touch with our own bodies, treating them as little more than obedient and useful machines. For many of us the body is a means to an end – to get us from one place to another, attract a mate, work the computer – but the mind is king. We depend on the body, we take it for granted, but we forget to listen to its messages.

Yet what about the intuitions that we experience through the body – the hunches we get, the awakening of interest, or the gut feeling that translates as wariness about a situation? These come to us first as physical sensations. By listening to this inner intelligence we can recognise and respond to our bodies' needs, spot the signs of physical tension and keep stress at bay.

eat well

What and how a person eats reveals as much about their relationship with their body and current stress levels as it does about their taste in food. When you are relaxed and in harmony with your body you listen to its messages and tune into its signals of hunger and satiety. By doing so you quite naturally eat the right amount, choosing a balanced combination of foods providing all the nutrients you need.

Stress, it need hardly be said, leads to poor eating habits. Stressed individuals, especially Type As, often eat on the run or in a distracted way, while doing other things. Even when they stop long enough to sit at the dining table, they often demolish their food at the double, finishing their plates before others are even halfway through. All this rushing down of their food, compounded by the fact that raised stress levels slow down the digestive process, causes indigestion and associated problems such as diarrhoea and constipation. Being stressed also makes some people liable to overeat, either because they turn to food for comfort when they feel stressed and depressed, or because they simply ignore their bodies' satiety signals. Conversely, by ignoring hunger signals, stressed individuals may undereat, or eat erratically, 'fuelling' their bodies instead with caffeine, nicotine or alcohol. When the body's hunger-satiety signals are constantly ignored the mechanism falls into disuse.

Fortunately our bodies are forgiving. By consciously regulating your food consumption and controlling the way you eat, by respecting and listening to your body, its natural intelligence and its instinctive desire for the nutrients it needs will reassert themselves.

Principles of eating well

- Sit down and eat three meals a day, or five smaller meals if you prefer. Don't go for more than a maximum of six or seven waking hours without eating, but do allow at least two or three hours between meals to give the body a chance to rest and digest, and for you to experience hunger in between meals.
- Don't rush your meals. Take your time, relax and enjoy your food. When you eat slowly, taking small mouthfuls and chewing well, you feel more satisfied and do not overeat.
- Make sure you eat a balanced and varied diet, including at least five portions of fresh fruit or vegetables, raw or lightly cooked, each day, to provide essential vitamins and minerals; three or four helpings of carbohydrates such as potatoes, rice, beans, pasta and bread, preferably whole grain; one or two portions of protein such as fish (eat two or three portions of oily fish, such as salmon, tuna or sardines, a week), meat, cheese, eggs, tofu, beans and nuts; a moderate amount

25

of fat, the best sources being vegetable oils such as olive oil, and fish oils (see above).

● Cut out or cut down on fatty foods and sugary snacks. Go for crunchy apples and raw vegetables such as celery and carrot sticks when you fancy a snack.

● Drink alcohol in moderation and avoid alcoholic binges. A glass or two of red wine is known to protect against heart disease. More can cause health problems such as liver and kidney disease. The recommended weekly limit for women is 14 units, 21 for men, spread out over the week.

● Limit caffeine to two or three cups of coffee, or five or six cups of tea, a day. If you are sensitive to caffeine, avoid it altogether. A good cuppa helps you unwind and relax, and tea is also a good source of antioxidants, which protect against heart disease and some forms of cancer. Caffeine, present in tea, coffee and cola, gives you a boost by stimulating the central nervous system, making you more alert. However, it can increase your stress levels and keep you awake, especially if drunk after mid-afternoon.

● Drink plenty of water, at least eight glasses a day, and more if you live or work in a centrally heated or air-conditioned home or office. Water flushes out impurities and waste products from the system, keeps body, hair and skin hydrated and healthy, and aids digestion.

● Indulge yourself occasionally.

● Never get stressed about what you are, or are not, eating!

perfect your posture

One of the greatest favours you can do yourself is to stop slouching and to stand straight, walk tall and sit up. Good posture

- opens up the airways, allowing you to breathe freely and deeply – fundamental to relieving stress
- increases energy levels and vitality
- supports your head correctly, making you feel lighter and more relaxed
- makes you look and feel more confident
- makes you appear younger, slimmer and in better shape.

Unfortunately, few people think about the way they sit or stand until severe pain in the back, shoulders and neck makes them all too aware of it. Back pain is becoming increasingly widespread in the West, second only to the common cold as a cause of days missed from work, and much of it the direct result of poor posture. An inactive lifestyle and long hours sitting hunched over keyboards, slumped in car seats and sofas cause tension, stiffness, stress and often irreversible damage to the spine. Slouching also leads to depleted energy levels and a negative outlook on life.

Beat back pain before it happens and reverse the effects of poor postural habits by developing an inner awareness of how you hold yourself and learning how to sit, stand and move with perfect posture. Learn to scan your body mentally, and to sit and stand correctly with the Body Check (pp. 62 and 102). Practise any of the sitting postures recommended for meditation (p. 36), and any of the exercise sequences such as the Sun Salutations (p. 48).

get moving

Taking regular exercise is the single most important thing you can do to promote physical and mental fitness and to keep stress at bay. Exercise cuts your risk of heart attacks, helps prevent osteoporosis, and can delay the onset of Alzheimer's disease. It makes you sleep better, boosts your energy, raises self-esteem, and ensures you look and feel great. So why do so most of us do so little?

Lack of time is one of the main reasons. But what if you could get all the benefits in just ten minutes?

In the past experts have recommended that adults should all be doing at least thirty minutes' continuous sweat-your-socks-off aerobic activity at least three times a week. But traditional guidelines have been superseded by the latest research, which recommends that we should accumulate twenty to thirty minutes of moderate physical activity most days a week. Even better news for the time-impoverished is that you do not have to do it all in one go. It can be done in two or three ten-minute sessions, which makes it much easier to achieve.

Ten-minute sessions are ideal not only if you have little time to spare (or little inclination!), but if you are currently not used to exercising. Experience shows that you are much more likely to stick with an exercise routine if you do not try to do too much, too soon. The hardest thing is to get started, but bear in mind that any activity counts. Incorporating simple exercise routines into your daily life can be just as beneficial as anything you can do at the gym, and there's little to be gained from pounding away at a treadmill if you are screaming with boredom – or comatose – after a few minutes. Forget it, and find something that engages your mind as well as your body. The slow, controlled movements of t'ai chi, pilates and above all yoga, mother of all exercise, are ideal for relieving both. Do ten minutes of stretching at home while you watch your favourite television programme, or work out with an exercise video. Put on some dance music and move to the beat.

regular exercise makes you sleep better, boosts your energy, raises self-esteem, and ensures you look and feel great

the latest research recommends that we should accumulate twenty to thirty minutes of moderate physical activity most days

28

Walking is one of the best all-round forms of exercise and the easiest to fit into even the busiest of schedules. Make a habit of ditching the car and walking or cycling for any distance less than a mile, or get off the bus, train or taxi a mile or two before the office or your home and take a brisk ten-minute walk. Three hours' walking a week – less than half an hour a day, which you can break into ten-minute slots – not only relieves stress, but has the added benefit that it cuts your risk of heart disease by 40 per cent.

Ideally, you should combine aerobic activity – exercise such as swimming, running and fast walking, that gets you perspiring and the heart pumping – with stretching exercises to maintain and increase flexibility, and weight-bearing activities, such as walking or jogging, in order to tone and strengthen the muscles. Many of the exercise sequences found later in this book, for example the Sun Salutations (p. 48), a personal favourite, combine all three.

your daily exercise can be done in two or three ten-minute sessions, which makes it much easier to achieve

get enough sleep

Time was when it was totally uncool to admit to more than five or six hours' sleep a night. Burning the candle at both ends – late nights in clubs, early morning breakfast meetings – was the hallmark of the seriously successful. But ill-health, premature ageing, depression, stress and burn-out have got the better of the chronically sleep-deprived, and sleep has once more reclaimed its rightful place as nature's great healer. Long nights of uninterrupted, restorative sleep are now acknowledged as a sign of the truly dynamic and creative, one of the surest ways to get to, and stay at, the top.

There is much you can do to ensure a good night's kip, but first, how much sleep do you need to function at optimum levels? Although needs vary from one individual to another, it is best to aim for eight hours of sound sleep a night. If you find yourself regularly waking naturally, and feeling refreshed, after less sleep than that, then your sleep requirement is less. If your sleep is interrupted or you are unwell, or you still feel tired after eight hours' quality sleep, you may need more. Beware, though, of trying to make up for a week's lost sleep at the weekend. For a start, a sleep debt of say an hour or two a day is difficult to pay off with one or two lie-ins unless you fancy spending virtually the entire weekend in bed. And if you do, you throw your body clock out of sync with its workaday needs. On top of that, on the days you sleep in you are likely to feel groggy and lethargic, have a headache, and to need at least three cups of strong coffee to get you going. Getting into a regular sleep routine – going to bed and waking up at regular times, with enough sleep in between – is the best way to relax and feel good.

getting into a regular sleep routine is the best way to relax and feel good

If you have difficulty in getting to sleep (taking more than twenty minutes), or you find yourself waking in the night with problems turning over in your mind, use meditative and other techniques to switch off after work, and make time to wind down before you go to bed (see p. 112).

Ten ways to a better night's sleep

● Create a restful environment in your bedroom. Make it a work-free, television-free zone and clear the clutter. Keep it as quiet and dark as possible, and neither too hot nor too cold: 16–18°C is ideal.

● Unless you are ill or exhausted, avoid afternoon naps.

● Ensure you have a comfortable, supportive mattress, and good head support. Too many pillows, or pillows that are too thin, strain the neck and cause headaches. Your head has the right support when the spinal section in the upper back is level with that of your neck.

● Relax and unwind before going to bed with a book, music, meditation or using one or more of the unwinding techniques and activities described on pp. 116–123. Prepare your body for sleep by developing them into a bedtime ritual, just as parents do for their children, doing the same things each night before bed.

● Base your evening meal on carbohydrate-rich foods such as baked potatoes, pasta and other cereals, and avoid heavy meals close to bedtime. Aim to eat your last meal of the day at least two hours before you go to bed.

● Caffeine is a stimulant that can keep you awake at night. Avoid tea, coffee, cola and even hot chocolate after 6p.m., earlier if you are especially sensitive to caffeine. Take milky drinks and herbal infusions instead.

● Avoid alcoholic nightcaps. Although alcohol can make you drowsy it interferes with sleep patterns, making you wake in the night, and causes dehydration and headaches.

● Take regular exercise, but not too close to bedtime.

● Try alternative remedies such as herbal medicine or aromatherapy. The herb valerian is commonly used to relieve stress and insomnia; or try sprinkling a few drops of an essential oil such as lavender in your bath or on to your pillow.

● If you wake in the night and cannot get back to sleep, get up and do something relaxing such as reading. If worries and problems are keeping you awake, offload them by writing them down or making lists of things to deal with the following day. Go back to bed when you feel sleepy.

mind and spirit

Relentlessly turning things over in your mind, unable to switch off, is a classic characteristic of stress. Looking after your body and taking regular physical exercise helps keep stress at bay, but you also need to make time for mental retreat.

A traditional way to calm the mind is through the ancient practice of meditation. Simple techniques such as awareness of your breathing, repeating a mantra or visualization, all act as gateways into the inner space, where the mind becomes quiet.

When the mind is at rest your innate and instinctive powers of self-healing come into play, and the stress response is reversed.

breathe easy
and relax

Awareness and regulation of the breathing process is not only an effective means of achieving mental and physical health and relaxation, but is believed by many to be a powerful tool in spiritual development. In fact, the way we breathe is considered so important in yoga that an entire branch of it is devoted to the art and science of breath control. The breathing process is also an important factor in meditation, and many forms of meditation involve focusing on the breath.

Children instinctively breathe healthily, but without our being aware of it we tend to breathe less efficiently as we become adult, using only the upper part of the chest. Generally when we are calm and relaxed we breathe deeply, in a slow and rhythmic fashion. When anxious and stressed we breathe faster, with shallow, irregular breaths sometimes punctuated by gasps as our bodies strive to increase the supply of oxygen. If this pattern of breathing continues unchecked it becomes a habit, which in turn makes us more nervous and agitated, and a vicious circle is established. Prolonged or extreme stress can result in overbreathing, or hyperventilation, which can cause dizziness and fainting, and trigger panic attacks.

simply by becoming aware of your breathing you can begin to reverse bad habits and train yourself to breathe correctly

33

Simply by becoming aware of your breathing you can begin to reverse bad habits and train yourself to breathe correctly. The breathing techniques described in Part 3 will rapidly relieve stress and still your mind in preparation for practising meditation or creative visualization.

meditate

Meditation has been practised for thousands of years by those searching for spiritual enlightenment, but one of the main reasons for its popularity today is that a proven side-effect is a marked improvement in both mental and physical health. Above all it is an effective antidote to stress.

Dubbed 'the relaxation response', meditation has been found to stem the flow of stress hormones and produce a response that is the reverse of the fight–flight, or stress, response. Regular meditation is accompanied by a significant decrease in heart rate, lowering of blood pressure, a calming of the nervous system and an improvement in all kinds of stress-related disorders such as depression, migraine and insomnia.

The beauty of meditation is that it is easy to learn and you can do it anywhere and at any time. All you need is ten minutes in a quiet place where you will not be disturbed, once or twice a day. First thing in the morning, when your mind is uncluttered by the events of the day, is the ideal time to meditate, but you can meditate at any convenient time. For lasting results you need to practise regularly, preferably daily.

A variety of different techniques of meditation are described in Part 3. Experiment a little to find out what works best for you. If possible, remove shoes and loosen any tight clothing before starting to meditate. Factors common to all the techniques in this book are:

Posture

A stable posture in which you can sit securely and keep still comfortably for ten minutes – or more if you wish to meditate for longer – with your spine straight but relaxed, is the foundation of meditation. The classic meditative posture is the lotus position, in which the legs are folded over one another. Alternatives are the half lotus or the 'perfect posture', but many people are more comfortable sitting in a simple cross-legged position on the floor, with a cushion beneath them for support, or kneeling. If none of these is comfortable for you, lie flat on the floor in the 'corpse position' and meditate in that position or sit upright on a straight-backed chair with your feet flat on the floor and your lower legs perpendicular. By holding any of these postures steadily your breathing will become steadier, your mind will become quieter, and meditation will happen more easily.

Breathing

For meditation your breathing should be natural, not forced or controlled. Breathe through your nose, not your mouth, and allow your breathing to become steadier of its own accord as your mind becomes still. If, during meditation, different breathing patterns such as breath retention happen spontaneously, do not worry. Just allow them to take place without interference.

Meditation focus

Most forms of meditation involve focusing attention on a particular object, image or sound – for example, silently repeating a mantra, gazing at a candle, concentrating on the space between your eyebrows or simply observing your breath as it comes in and goes out. Other kinds of meditation involve an opening out of attention, becoming aware of whatever is happening both internally and in your external surroundings, and just being in the moment, allowing thoughts to come and go without interference.

Attitude

When people complain that they cannot meditate, this is usually because they get caught up in all the thoughts and feelings that keep rushing around in their minds and then try forcibly to suppress them. Instead of worrying about thoughts and images that arise during meditation, simply notice them without comment and gently bring your attention back to the focus of your meditation.

the lotus
flower is the
symbol of
spiritual
unfolding

the positions

▼ Lotus

The lotus position, in which the Buddha is classically depicted, is the ideal posture for meditation, so much so that it has become its very symbol. The legs are locked together, providing a stable base from which the meditator will neither topple over nor fall asleep, and no effort is required to maintain the position. Although very relaxing once hips, knees and ankles have become sufficiently flexible, the posture is invariably uncomfortable to begin with, particularly if you are accustomed only to sitting in a chair. Never force your legs into this position.

Instructions

Sit on the floor with your legs stretched out in front of you. Bend your right knee and take hold of your right foot, placing it at the top of the left thigh so that the heel presses into the abdomen. Then in the same way bend your left leg and place your left foot on top of the right thigh. The soles of your feet should be turned up and both knees should touch the ground. Your back should be straight from the base of the spine to the neck, the back of your head in line with the base of your spine, and your abdomen relaxed. The hands are placed on the knees, palms up, with the thumb and first finger touching. Alternatively they can be placed between the heels, one over the other. Begin by holding the position for up to a minute, gradually increasing the length of time you stay in it.

In the classic lotus the left leg is placed on top, but to develop equal flexibility on both sides it is best to reverse the roles of the legs regularly. This applies to all cross-legged postures.

36

◀ Half lotus

If you find it difficult to sit in the full lotus you may like to start with the half lotus.

Instructions

Sit on the floor with your legs stretched out in front of you. Bend your left knee and place your left foot beneath the right thigh as close as possible to your buttocks. Then bend your right knee and place your right foot on top of the left thigh, as in the full lotus. Again, both knees should touch the ground and your back should be kept straight. Place your hands as for the full lotus and regularly reverse the positions of your legs.

37

▶ Perfect posture

This is another classic meditative pose, easier to achieve than the lotus posture, but again a position of great stability.

Instructions

Sit on the floor with your legs stretched out in front of you. Bend the left knee and place the left foot against the perineum (the soft flesh between the anus and the genitals). Then bend the right knee and place the heel against the pubic bone. With the sole of the foot upturned, tuck the toes in between the calf and thigh of the left leg. Buttocks, thighs and knees should all rest on the floor. Place your hands as for the lotus posture, and regularly reverse the positions of the legs.

▶ Simple cross-legged position

This is an easy position for most people. As with all meditation positions, the back should be straight but not rigid, and the abdomen relaxed.

Instructions

Sit with your buttocks on a cushion or blanket and cross your legs so that your feet are on the floor beneath your knees and your head, neck and trunk are in a straight line. Place your hands on your knees or in your lap and regularly reverse the positions of the legs.

◀ Kneeling

Many people find this a good alternative to the simple cross-legged position, as it is easier to keep the spine straight and relaxing for tired legs.

Instructions

With your back upright, kneel down keeping your knees together. Separate the heels and bring the big toes together so that you sit on the insides of your feet. If your buttocks do not comfortably reach your feet, insert a cushion – or two if necessary – between them. Place your hands on your knees.

Alternatively, keeping your knees together, set the feet apart and sit in between them, using cushions beneath your buttocks if they do not reach the floor. Place your hands on your knees.

◀ Sitting on a chair

If you are unable to sit on the floor, sit with your back straight but relaxed on a chair or stool with a firm seat.

Instructions

Place your feet flat on the floor, hip width apart, with your knees directly above them and your hands in your lap. Placing a small cushion at the back of the chair so you are sitting on the front edge of it encourages upright posture and the correct distribution of weight.

▼ Corpse position

A position for anyone who has trouble sitting upright. It is also incredibly relaxing and plays a part in many of the exercises and techniques in this book.

Instructions

Lie flat on the floor, preferably with a mat or folded blanket beneath you, or on a firm mattress. Separate your legs slightly and allow your feet to fall outwards to the sides. Move your arms slightly away from your body and rest your hands on the floor with the palms up. This position is also used for physical relaxation, and can also be used before or after meditation in any of the sitting positions.

be positive

It may be a cliché, but to a large extent life really is what you make it. Your attitude to everyday problems and issues can make all the difference to your experience of life. Never underestimate the power of your own mind. Research has shown over and over again that optimistic people with a positive outlook on life are healthier and live longer, and tend to have more stable relationships and better-paid jobs, than their negaholic counterparts. Pessimists make their own lives miserable and they drag others down with them. Alter your mindset from negative to positive – see your glass as half full rather than half empty – and you give yourself the potential for a healthier, happier and longer life, as well as helping yourself to deal more effectively with life's difficulties.

convert to positive thinking with the affirmations suggested here, or create your own

40

Turn negatives into positives

Take time to become more aware of your thought processes – meditation often offers a perfect opportunity for this – and whenever you notice yourself talking or thinking in a negative way make a conscious effort to recast your thoughts in a positive light. See challenges and opportunities, not threats. Look for the good in others, yourself, and any situation you find yourself in instead of constantly finding fault.

Develop good coping and problem-solving strategies

Assume that troubles are temporary and that problems have solutions. Think through the alternatives when your mind is clear and you feel fresh, not when you are tired and in need of sleep. Even the most daunting of problems can be broken down into manageable chunks.

use affirmations

Affirmations are strong, positive statements – powerful tools for boosting self-esteem and confidence. Through repetition of any particular affirmation the subconscious mind comes to accept its message, and negative self-talk is replaced by positive images and ideas. The most famous affirmation, coined by Émile Coué, the French psychotherapist and pioneer of autosuggestion is this: *Every day, in every way, I am getting better and better.* This affirmation lies at the heart of Couéism, as his system became known. Couéism flourished in the 1920s and, much as sceptics may laugh, it works. Thousands of people have experienced positive changes in their lives as a result of using his formula.

Even though most of the time we are completely unaware of it, our minds are constantly active. Different thoughts, ideas and feelings incessantly rush in, as anyone who practices meditation soon finds out. By dispassionately observing your mind and its inner dialogue rather than engaging in it, you become aware of destructive patterns of thought that influence how you feel and what is happening in your life. Affirmations allow you to replace negative internal chatter and thoughts with positive ones, a process that can transform your attitudes and change your life.

You can create affirmations to achieve anything you want, to improve any kind of situation, and to combat any kind of stress: the fear of failure, lack of confidence or self-esteem, pain, anger and so on. Use them while they feel right, and create new ones as your mood and circumstances change. Affirmations can be general or specific, are best kept short and simple, and should always be:

- positive rather than negative: *I am relaxed and calm* not *I am no longer stressed and exhausted.*
- stated in the present tense, not the future: *I have a perfect relationship with...* not *My relationship with... is getting better.*

Affirmations can be repeated like a mantra at any time of day – while travelling to work, preparing a meal, having a bath. Here are a few to get you started:

- *Whatever happens in my life, I can handle it.*
- *I take responsibility for my life, from my innermost thoughts to my outer reality.*
- *My life is filled with an abundance of love, peace and joy.*

And of course:

- *I take ten minutes to relax whenever I need to.*

ten-minute

stress-busters

rise and morning

A good night's sleep is essential to getting
a fresh start and feeling good the following
day. On average adults function best on a
regular seven and a half to eight hours'
sleep a night. Less and you are likely to be
tired, irritable and inefficient; more and you
feel woolly-headed and inert. If you wake
up naturally, without an alarm, feeling
completely rested, then you are getting the
right amount of sleep. If you are getting less
sleep than you need – and stress is the
enemy of sleep – then follow the tips to
a better night's sleep on p. 31.

Most of the techniques and strategies in
this section can be practised at any time of

shine: routines

day, but they are particularly suited to the early hours. How the morning begins influences your entire day and it is well worth the effort of getting up that little bit earlier to get a head start. Even the way you wake up can make a difference. The shrill ring of a conventional alarm clock is a rather brutal way to start the day, but there are plenty of soothing alternatives on offer. Awaken gently to the sound of bird song, ocean waves or mantras with the new generation of alarm clocks, or to your favourite sounds using a CD player with a built-in alarm.

Once awake, try to find time for a little stretching, either in bed or once you are up.

If you feel a bit groggy first thing or, heaven forbid, morning-afterish, there's nothing to beat a little early-morning yoga. The Sun Salutations (p. 48), traditionally performed at sunrise, are possibly the best exercise sequence in the entire universe. A few rounds at the start of the day will make you feel completely energized and raring to go. Morning is also the ideal time for breathing exercises and meditation.

So get the day off to a flying start with a little stretching and flexing to loosen the joints, a little meditation to get centred, and a proper breakfast to keep your energy levels up and boost concentration. If you are lucky enough to live within walking distance of work, then ditch the car and avoid public transport. Make the most of a brisk walk to get fit and relax.

breath-awareness
meditation

You can meditate at any time at all, but first thing in the morning, when your mind is at its clearest and most uncluttered, is ideal. Later on it may take a while to turn your attention away from the events and preoccupations of the day. Practising a few rounds of bellows-breathing (see p. 114) is a very effective way to still your mind before you begin.

How to meditate
In a quiet and peaceful room or corner, sit upright in a simple cross-legged position, or in any of the meditation positions illustrated on pages 36 to 39. Close your eyes and breathe naturally, and become aware of your breath as it comes in and goes out. If your mind wanders, don't worry. Just observe any thoughts and feeling that arise and allow them to come and go without getting caught up in them. Then gently bring your attention back to your breath.

To help still your mind you can use the *hamsa* mantra, a simple and natural technique of observing the breath as it flows in and out.

Hamsa (so'ham): 'I am that'
According to yogic literature, this sound, *hamsa*, is continuously repeated by every living being, whether they are aware of it or not, and for this reason it is called the 'natural mantra'. The sequence *hamsa-hamsa-hamsa* can also be heard as *so'ham-so'ham-so'ham*, Sanskrit for 'I am that', when the order of the syllables is reversed.

To meditate using the *hamsa* mantra, listen to the sound of your breath as it comes in and out. As you breathe in, hear the sound *ham* (pronounced *hum*) and as you breathe out, *sa* (*sah* or *so*). Focus your attention on the spaces between breaths – between *ham* and *sa*, and between *sa* and *ham*. Whatever thoughts and feelings arise, just let them be without engaging with them. Once you experience the stillness in the centre of your being, you can let go of the *ham* and the *sa* and lose yourself in meditation.

Hamsa, so'ham

हंस । सोऽहम् ॥

sun salutations

One of the very best sequences of movements ever devised, the Sun Salutation is a graceful series of twelve yoga postures that are traditionally performed at sunrise, as the name suggests. A condensed yoga programme in itself, the sequence oxygenates the blood and energises the whole system, bringing increased suppleness to the spine and strengthening and toning the entire body.

Performed fairly rapidly on rising, the Sun Salutations sweep the sleep clean out of your system and provide an invigorating start to the day. If you do them before a full programme of yoga postures – or any physical exercise – the series provides an excellent warm-up. Performed slowly, the Sun Salutations relieve physical tension and make a great way to relax and unwind.

There are many variations of the Sun Salutations. The version described here is the one most often found in yogic literature, and one of the easiest to learn.

◀ Position 1

Stand upright with your feet together, weight evenly spread over your soles, and bring your palms together in front of your chest. Breathe out.

◀ Position 2

Breathing in, stretch your arms up and slightly back, palms facing forward.

▶ Position 3

Breathing out, bend forwards from the hips, placing your palms flat on the floor beside your feet and bringing your face as close to your knees as you can. You may need to bend your knees in this position to begin with.

▶ Position 4

Without moving your hands or your left foot, breathe in and stretch back with your right leg, placing the knee on the floor and curling the toes under. Your left knee should then be above your left ankle. Arch your back and look up.

▶ Position 5

Holding your breath, bring your left leg back alongside the right, supporting your body on your hands and toes. Head, back, legs and heels should all be in a straight line.

▼ Position 6

Breathing out, bend your arms and lower your knees, chest and chin to the floor, keeping the elbows high and the hands firmly down.

◀ Position 7

Breathing in, lower the hips to the floor and slide forward so that your toes point back. Straighten your arms, lift your chest and take your head back.

▼ Position 8

Breathing out, curl your toes under and lift your hips up into an upside-down V shape. Keeping your legs straight, push back on your heels, trying to place your feet flat on the floor. Drop your head in between your arms.

▶ Position 9

Breathing in, bring your right leg forward between your
hands and at the same time lower your left knee to
the floor. Arch your back and look up. This is the
mirror image of position 4.

◀ Position 10

Breathing out, bring the left leg in line with the
right, and assume position 3 again.

◀ Position 11

Breathing in, extend your arms up and back, repeating position 2.

▶ Position 12

Breathing out, lower your arms to your sides or, if you are performing another round, resume the starting position.

• Repeat the sequence leading with the left leg in positions 4 and 9 to complete one full round of the Sun Salutation.

Begin with one round, practising the sequence slowly and carefully, perfecting each posture and moving as smoothly as you can from one position to the next, gradually adding a round a day until you have built up to 12 rounds.

 After completing the Sun Salutations, lie down for a few minutes in the corpse position (see p. 39). Close your eyes and allow your breathing rhythm to return to normal, then follow with a few rounds of abdominal breathing (see p. 113).

bathroom bends

Find new uses for your bath towels and bathroom surfaces and combine your morning ablutions with this balanced sequence of bending and stretching exercises which improve circulation, release morning stiffness and mentally prepare you for the day.

▼ Shoulder release

This is particularly good for easing stiff shoulders, for upper-back problems and for improving posture.

Instructions

1 Holding a towel in your right hand, extend your right arm straight upwards, then bend at the elbow and bring your hand to the centre of your upper back.

2 Extend the left arm horizontally to the side, then stretch it down, bend at the elbow and reach up with your hand. Catch the towel as close to your right hand as you can manage, and hold for 30 seconds.

3 Repeat on the other side.

Focus points

● Keep your chest lifted and your tailbone in.
● Stretch your elbows vertically away from one another.
● Work towards reducing the distance between your hands. If you can catch your fingers together, or even your wrists, you can dispense with the towel.

◀ **Chest opener**

As the name suggests, this opens your chest, relieves stiffness in your shoulders and upper back, and improves your posture, particularly if you spend a lot of time in front of a screen. Practised regularly, it will improve your whole breathing pattern and lift your mood.

Instructions

1 Hold the towel in both hands, approximately two shoulder widths apart, and keeping your arms straight, breathe in and take your arms up above your head, keeping the towel stretched.

2 Breathe out and take the towel over your head and round to the back.

3 Breathe in and lift the towel back up.

4 Breathing out, lower the arms over to the front so that you have made a full circle.

5 Repeat up to five times.

Focus points

● Make the movement soft, slow and fluid.
● Keep your chest lifted, your shoulders down and your tailbone in.
● If you do not feel the stretch, bring your hands closer together.

▼ Right-angle bend

This stretches the arms and shoulders, relieves stiffness in the back, and stretches the legs.

Instructions

1 Place your hands on the edge of a support at roughly hip level, such as a basin, shoulder width apart.

2 Walk back until your arms are straight, your back extended and your legs vertical.

3 Move your hips back away from your hands.

4 Pressing your weight down into your heels, pull up your thighs and knees.

5 Stretch forward into your fingertips, extending the full length of your back. Hold for 5–8 seconds.

Focus points

● Keep your hands in line with the rest of your arms, don't allow the wrists to drop.
● Draw your abdomen towards your back.
● Keep your head in line with your arms, so the crown of your head is moving towards your hands.

▼ Back release

This keeps your back supple, opens your chest, and brings energy and vitality.

Instructions

1 Start from the Right-angle position (opposite). Breathe in and, keeping your arms straight, bring your hips towards your support and lift your head.

2 Lift your heels and, keeping your legs straight, move your tailbone in.

3 Move your shoulders down, lift your chest and, breathing out, look towards the ceiling. Hold for 5–8 seconds.

4 Breathe out and return to the Right-angle position.

Focus points

● Take your shoulders back and down before looking up.
● If you feel any pain in your neck do not look up.
● Allow the movement to be fluid.

57

◀ Knee bends

This energizes, strengthens and releases tension in legs, ankles and feet.

Instructions

1 Stand with your knees together and your hands resting on your basin or another support with space beneath it.

2 Breathe in and lift your heels as high as possible.

3 Breathe out and bend your knees slowly until your thighs are horizontal. Hold for 5–10 seconds, or longer if you can, but without holding your breath.

4 Breathe in and come up. Take your heels down as you breathe out, and repeat five times.

Focus points
● Keep your head and chest lifted and your shoulders down.
● Once lifted, try to keep your heels high as you bend your knees.
● No shoes or slippers, please!

▶ Leg up

This exercise will stretch and strengthen your legs, release hips and shoulders and extend the spine.

You will need a support – a stool, loo seat or even your basin if you are flexible – for one foot. The height of your support should be such that you can straighten both legs when standing as in the illustration. Place books on your support to adjust the height if necessary, but do not take the foot too high to begin with.

Instructions

1 Stand with your feet together facing your support. Bend your knees and then lift your right leg, placing your foot on the support. Straighten both legs.

2 Lift your chest and the crown of your head, extending the spine and the back of the neck upwards.

3 If you can, interlace your fingers and extend your arms up above your head turning your palms to face the ceiling. Hold for 30 seconds.

4 Repeat lifting the left leg.

Focus points

● See that your standing foot points straight forward in the direction of your support.
● Rest the back of the heel, not the back of the ankle on your support.
● If you cannot extend your arms upwards keep your hands on your hips and your shoulders down.

59

Wake up to the wonders of hydrotherapy

Create your own home spa in the privacy of your bathroom and wake yourself up to the wonders of hydrotherapy. Water is the very essence of life – without it we cannot survive more than two or three days. These simple techniques refresh tired eyes, and leave you totally energized and ready to start the day.

Eye splashing

Keeping your eyes closed, alternately splash them with hot (not too hot!) and cold water, about twenty-five splashes of each, then repeat.

If you have any form of eye disease or infection, or very poor sight, then use hot and cold compresses instead. Fold a soft clean cloth or flannel kept specially for the purpose into a pad large enough to cover the eyes and surrounding area. Immerse it in very warm water, squeeze out the excess water and apply the cloth to your closed eyelids until it has cooled. Follow with a cold flannel, then repeat the whole process.

Bright eyes

If you wake in the morning with puffy eyes, keep a flask of hot water by your bed, drink a glass first thing, then lie back in the corpse position (see p. 39) for 10 minutes. The hot water helps to kick-start the kidneys and draw out retained water from the delicate tissue around the eyes. As you lie back, close your eyes and become aware of your breathing, without altering the natural flow of the breath. If your body feels tense, practise deep muscle relaxation (see p. 82)

Shower power

If you're man – or woman – enough, try extending the power of hydrotherapy to your morning ablutions, or any other time you need a quick pick-me-up, using alternating shower temperatures. The hot and cold contrast will tone you up, get your circulation going, stimulate your internal organs, boost your immune system, and leave your whole body tingling with pleasure and raring to go.

Start with the shower warm for a few minutes, then turn the temperature down as cool as you can bear for half a minute or so, then back to warm. Repeat two or three times, finishing up with cold water. Wrap yourself up, preferably in warm towels, pat yourself dry and relax for a few minutes.

Now you are dried and revitalized, channel your new-found energy with a quick burst of exercise: the bathroom bends (see p. 54) are tailor-made.

make time for breakfast

If you rely on strong black coffee to get you up in the morning, and more to keep going until lunchtime, it may be time for a change.

Caffeine gives you a temporary lift, but too much lowers energy and raises anxiety and stress levels; and a huge body of research shows that by skipping breakfast you set yourself up for a mid-morning energy slump and put yourself at a distinct disadvantage compared with your breakfast-eating friends and colleagues. Eating a proper breakfast not only boosts your energy levels, it boosts your brain power too, and this is proven by performance in physical and mental tests. Breakfast eaters have better concentration, better memories and better moods than breakfast skippers. *And* they are slimmer.

The message is clear: make time for breakfast. If you can't face it first thing in the morning, postpone it for an hour or so to give sluggish systems time to get going and get your digestive juices flowing.

Of course what you eat is as important as when you eat it. To beat the mid-morning blues – and munchies – you are best going for foods such as cereals, which release energy slowly into the bloodstream. A bowl of your favourite cereal with semi-skimmed milk, plus some fresh fruit and yogurt, all washed down with a glass of fruit juice, makes a good quick breakfast that will keep you going until lunchtime. If you have more time, try porridge with raisins, honey and toasted sesame seeds, or whisk up a health-giving and power-packed smoothie in your blender: the combination of linseed, yogurt, milk, tofu and blueberries is especially beneficial for women, or try a simple mix of seasonal fruits, for example banana, peach and apple, blended together with milk. The combinations and permutations are endless – and there are some excellent recipe books to choose from. If it's breakfast on the move or in the office, a cereal bar and a piece of fruit are one of the best alternatives.

A word about caffeine... If there's nothing you enjoy more than a good cuppa or cappuccino, then go ahead and enjoy. They will do you more good than harm, and tea in particular contains powerful antioxidants that protect against heart disease and cancer, among other things. To release these, tea must be steeped for at least three minutes, and is best drunk black. However, any benefits of caffeine are associated with a consumption equivalent of up to three cups of coffee (filtered) a day, or about six cups of tea. So cut out all the mindless cups of tea and coffee that you have out of habit rather than enjoyment, and avoid drinking tea at meal times as it can interfere with iron absorption.

61

de-stress

A sedentary lifestyle with long hours spent at a desk is the lot of many office workers, from the most junior to the company chairman or woman. This, combined with pressures of work, causes both mental and physical tension which it is important to release.

When you are busy and preoccupied with work it's easy to miss the signs of tension building up. To avoid stress creeping up on you unawares, give yourself regular 'health checks' and break up long periods of inactivity with movement to prevent muscles stiffening and joints seizing up.

Get into the habit of using the body check several times a day. It is a rapid way to tune into the body, correct poor posture, scan for physical tension and relax. With practice it

at your desk

can be done in just a few moments while sitting at your desk. For ten-minute stress relief combine it with toe-to-head relaxation of each part of the body.

The regular practice of eye exercises followed by relaxation using the technique of palming is highly recommended for anyone who works long hours at a screen or suffers from eye discomfort. The workaholic's workout is a series of easy routines specially devised to release stiffness and tension in the main problem areas – neck, back, shoulders and so on – while at your desk or in other small spaces. The exercises can be done together as a ten-minute sequence, or you can check your body for tension and zoom in on the hot spots!

the body check: sitting

Inactivity combined with poor posture – sitting hunched up in your chair, bending over paperwork – is a sure-fire recipe for a stiff body, tense muscles, spinal damage and back pain. And that's just for starters. Necks and shoulders feel the strain, as do heads, brains and eyes also, especially when glued to a screen for long stretches of time.

Use the body check at regular intervals when you are sitting for long periods to correct posture, check for tension spots and relax. Sitting well has a huge impact on your overall well-being, and is the starting point for the exercises which follow. Good sitting posture not only reduces stiffness, aches and pains but, even more important, keeps your chest open so you breathe more efficiently.

The version of the body check given here is in essence the same as the standing version (see p. 102). Once you have got the hang of it, the body check can be done almost anywhere – at your desk, in the bathroom, in a waiting room – to get in touch with your body's inner wisdom and become receptive to its needs.

Instructions

1 Sit with your feet firm and flat on the floor (place books or telephone directories beneath them if necessary), hip width apart, knees directly above them and slightly lower than your hips. Alternatively if comfortable you can sit on your chair in the lotus or half lotus position (see p. 36). Rest your hands in your lap or allow them to hang loosely by your sides. Close your eyes to help you focus inwards.

2 Breathe in deeply, feeling your abdomen swell, your side ribs expand and the top of your chest lift. Straighten your back, lengthening your spine and extending the back of your neck without tensing the muscles. Keep your chin tucked in.

3 Breathing out, lower your shoulders and draw them back gently, pressing your shoulder blades into your back.

4 Take one or two more deep breaths, stretching and elongating your spine upwards with each inhalation, keeping your shoulders down and back, and tucking your chin in. The weight of your upper body should now be centred over your sitting bones, your abdomen back and drawn up. Imagine a golden thread in the centre of your spine extending from the base vertically upwards through the crown of your head, gently drawing you up.

5 Hold the posture comfortably and, breathing naturally, consciously relax your whole body, being sure to soften and relax your face, jaw and tongue, which holds a lot of tension.

6 If you have time, relax each part of the body in turn with the help of autosuggestion. Focus your attention on the body part and mentally give it the message to relax and let go, then moving on to the next part: Left foot, relax; left calf, relax; left thigh, relax; right foot, relax... and so forth right up to your scalp.

7 Mentally scan your body from the tips of your toes to the crown of your head, noting any tension spots. These can often be a clue to inner conflict that needs resolution. Where there is tension in your body, visualize yourself breathing into it. Breathe in relaxation, breathe out tension.

8 Open your eyes and keep on sitting this way for a few minutes.

Your body should now feel poised, relaxed and centred. If you find sitting this way a strain it is probably due to weak back muscles, resulting from poor posture. Through regular practice they will strengthen and sitting well will become habitual.

eye relief

Sore eyes and blurry vision are hazards of office life, and if your job involves staring at a screen for more than three hours a day you are very likely to suffer from some form of eye strain and discomfort. To relieve eyestrain:

- blink often to moisten dry eyes
- take frequent breaks from the computer
- do eye exercises daily
- rest and relax your eyes by palming (see p. 85).

Just like any other muscles, the eye muscles need regular exercise. These exercises strengthen the muscles, relieve and help prevent eyestrain, and will improve your sight if practised once or twice a day.

▼ Clock watching
Instructions

1 Sit with your feet firm and flat on the floor, your back straight, your chest lifted and your shoulders rolling back. Alternatively, if comfortable, you can sit on your chair in the lotus or half lotus position (see p. 37). Rest your hands in your lap or allow them to hang loosely by your sides, and breathe normally throughout the exercise.

2 Imagine a huge clock (the old-fashioned sort with numbers and hands) in front of you a few feet away from your face. Without moving your head, look up at twelve o'clock then down to six o'clock, up to one o'clock then diagonally down to seven o'clock, to two o'clock then across to eight o'clock, and so on round the clock. Repeat each pair of opposites several times before going on to the next pair.

3 Repeat in the opposite direction.

4 Now move your eyes clockwise around the clock, beginning at 12.00, and coming full circle back again. Make slow circles for two or three rounds, then faster for another two or three rounds. Repeat in an anti-clockwise direction

▶ **Near–far focusing**
Instructions

1 Sitting as above, hold your forefinger up in front of your nose, about a foot away from you.

2 Focus first on your finger, then on the wall or on any object beyond (in the middle or far distance). Alternate your gaze to and fro, focusing as clearly as you are able, several times.

67

Palming

Palming (see p. 85) can be done on its own for a minute or two any time to refresh tired eyes, or used in conjunction with the eye exercises above.

the workaholic's workout

The exercises that follow together make up a ten-minute workout that you can do at your desk to relieve the stress hot spots – neck, back and shoulders – calm your mind and energize your entire system.

▶ Breathe into your shoulders

Shoulders, neck, upper back, wrists, elbows.

Moving in rhythm with your breath helps release tension and stiffness, improves concentration and increases energy levels. This exercise is particularly helpful for RSI (Repetitive Strain Injury) sufferers.

Instructions

1 Sit with your back straight, your chest lifted and your shoulders rolling back. Move your abdomen back and up, and your tailbone in. Have your feet hip distance apart with your toes pointing straight forward. If your feet are not firmly flat on the floor place books beneath them.

2 Interlace your fingers. Exhale and press the hands forwards horizontally away from your chest, turning your palms out and then straightening your arms.

3 Keeping your arms straight, inhale and extend the arms vertically above your head, moving your elbows in (see opposite).

4 Exhale, keep your hands above your head and bend the elbows out to the sides. Resting your hands on the crown of your head, take your shoulders down and extend the elbows away from one other.

5 Inhale and extend the arms above your head. Press the thumb side of your hand up higher than the little finger side.

6 Exhale and take your arms forward.

7 Repeat several times in a continuous movement, changing the interlace of your fingers halfway through so that the other hand is on top.

69

Focus points
● Keep your chest lifted, even when bringing your arms down.
● Breathe through your nose without holding your breath. Your breathing should be soft, slow, deep and rhythmic.

▶ Energizing chest opener

Chest, shoulders, upper back, neck.

  This position improves posture and increases energy by opening the chest. It relieves stiffness and tension in the shoulders, upper back and neck.

Instructions

1 Sit forward on your chair with your back straight and your feet hip distance apart. If your feet are not firmly flat on the floor, place books beneath them.

2 Place your hands on the back of your seat with your fingers pointing forwards. Take your shoulders down, point your elbows back and lift your chest.

3 Inhale and lift your chest to look up to the ceiling. Exhale. Hold for as long as you feel comfortable, lifting your chest with each inhalation, and maintaining the lift with each exhalation.

4 Inhale, keeping your chest lifted, come up and raise. Repeat twice.

Focus points

- Keep your shoulders back and down.
- Take your shoulder blades into the flesh of your back and down.
- If you feel any discomfort in your neck, do not hold the position.
- Take your abdomen towards your back; keep your tailbone in.

◀ **Unwind your spine**

Back, neck, shoulders, digestion, elimination.
This balancing exercise has a calming, restorative and energizing effect on your whole system.

Instructions

1 Sit with your back straight, your chest lifted and your shoulders rolling back. Move your abdomen back and up. Have your feet hip distance apart with your toes pointing straight forward. If your feet are not firmly flat on the ground place books beneath them.

2 Breathe in, extending the spine up.

3 Breathe out, turning to your right. Hold the back of your chair with your right hand. Bring your left hand to the outer right thigh.

4 Breathe in and lift further. Breathe out and turn further. Without forcing your neck, turn your head around to look behind you.

5 Breathe in and lift. As you breathe out come back to the front.

6 Repeat to the left, and repeat the whole cycle several times in one continuous flow. Try to turn a little farther each time.

71

Focus points

● Keep your weight even on both sitting bones and your thighs in place as you rotate the trunk.
● Keep your chest lifted through out and your spine extending throughout.
● Keep your face soft, teeth slightly apart.

▸ Ease your back

Back, hips, shoulders, head, neck, period pains, wind.
This forward bend calms the mind and releases stiffness in the lower back, neck and shoulders. It also relieves menstrual pain and eases abdominal tension and the discomfort of bloating and wind that go with it.

Instructions

1 Sit with your back straight and your feet wider than hip width, pointing forward. (Ladies with skirts can always do this on the loo seat!)

2 Make two fists and place them on either side of the lower abdomen. Inhale, lift the chest and with an exhalation fold over your fists, releasing your head and your shoulders towards the floor, and allowing your arms to rest on your thighs.

3 Stay in this position for 30 seconds or longer, breathing softly and releasing the back, shoulders and abdomen with each exhalation.

4 Inhale to come up.

Focus points

● When placing your fists, use them to scoop and lift up the flesh of the abdomen, creating more space between the abdomen and the thighs.
● When you are in the position, let your head hang heavily to the floor with your eyes closed.

▶ **Save your neck**

Neck and shoulders.

This exercise calms nerves and releases tension in the neck and across the top of the shoulders.

Instructions

1 Sit with your back straight and your chest lifted. Hold the seat of your chair with your left hand.

2 Inhale and turn your head slightly until your chin is over your right collar bone. Place your right hand on the crown of your head and gently draw your chin down as you exhale.

3 Hold for three soft, slow breaths, keeping the back straight and the chest lifted throughout.

4 Repeat on the other side.

Focus points

• Keep your face and tongue soft, with your teeth slightly apart.
• If you feel any discomfort do not hold.

73

time out

Time to yourself is key to dealing with stress, and the more hectic your life, the more you need it. The electronic revolution – email, laptops, mobile phones – means increasing numbers of people are constantly plugged in, able to work anywhere, anytime. This brings huge advantages and liberates us from the workplace, but the downside is that it means we are always available, never off duty. Boundaries between work and personal life become blurred or non-existent, with implications for health, happiness, relationships and stress levels.

Non-stop working and constant rushing around is counterproductive. However busy you are, schedule daily fixes of me-time into your day. Physically remove yourself from your working environment if you can – the lunch break presents the ideal opportunity for this – and go for a stroll or a run. If you cannot get away then switch off all forms of communication – electronic, telephonic or otherwise – for ten minutes. Deep relaxation (see p. 82) is a powerful way to refresh mentally and release physical tension throughout the entire body. Alternatively, you may prefer to unwind with some soothing music (see p. 78) or to try any of the other following ten-minute stress-relief suggestions.

Taking time out to relax recharges your batteries, keeps your life in balance, improves your health and makes you a more effective problem-solver. Last but not least, it makes you a much nicer person to be around!

lunch break

If you work indoors, especially in a sedentary job, make sure you get out at lunchtime even if only for a brisk walk. A change of environment and a bit of fresh air helps put problems in perspective and getting moving can make a huge difference not only by reducing your stress levels, but by boosting your fitness and energy levels.

10 minutes walking and jogging

Walking gets you as fit as running, provided you walk fast, and being outside has a beneficial effect on your whole psyche. Walk briskly for ten minutes, relaxing as you walk by taking deep breaths and walking in rhythm with your breathing, for example four steps to each inhalation, four to each exhalation. For more vigorous exercise alternate walking with jogging. Try to avoid busy, polluted roads and if possible take a scenic route or head for the nearest park, riverside or open space.

Spend time outdoors

In clement weather make yourself a picnic lunch, or visit the nearest sandwich shop and find a tranquil spot in a local park, garden square or on the banks of a river to eat it. Just being out in the open lowers stress levels, but natural landscapes, if there are any near your place of work, have a particularly calming effect. Practice the food meditation below.

Sit still for ten minutes contemplating your surroundings and absorbing yourself in nature. Become aware of all the sounds, shapes and colours around you, or focus on a particular feature such as a flower, leaf, tree or the sound of birdsong or flowing water. Visualize worries and stress being scattered by the wind or washed away.

Notice how you feel. Your breathing should now be smooth and even, mind and body energized and relaxed.

a change of environment and a bit of fresh air helps put problems in perspective

Retail therapy and flower power

(For non-addictive shoppers only: shopaholics, beware!)

It may seem an unlikely way to relieve stress, but love it or loathe it, shopping and window shopping is nationally one of our favourite ways to spend leisure time and relax. So if lunchtime means a trip to the shops to pick up the groceries, turn it into a therapeutic experience and indulge yourself in a little retail therapy.

Spend ten minutes browsing in your local book shop and pick out any books you that interest you. A good read will provide hours of enjoyable relaxation. Check out design, gadget, antique and second-hand shops for curios and objects. Visualize where you could put them, how you could use them. Mentally redecorate – it keeps your creative juices going. If fashion is your passion, sift through the rails and explore colours and combinations you would never normally wear. You don't have to buy. Wind up in the florist and treat yourself to a bunch of fresh, fragrant flowers. They are guaranteed to lift your spirits and will provide instant stress relief for days.

Food meditation

This slows you down, improves your digestion, and helps you relax. It also helps you reconnect with the sensuous joys of eating.

To practice food meditation sit somewhere where you will not be disturbed or distracted so you can focus on eating and observe the smells, textures and colours of the food on your plate. Then, taking small mouthfuls, chew your food slowly and thoroughly, rolling it around your mouth. Savour the enjoyment as delicious flavours fill your mouth and absorb yourself completely in the pleasures of eating and drinking.

If you tend to eat fast – a common type A characteristic – practising food meditation will help you create new habits of eating slowly and mindfully. However, to practise food meditation you do not need an entire meal. A bite or two will suffice. Try a piece of raw fruit or vegetable – cauliflower is a surprisingly good choice – or a piece of chocolate. If you completely absorb yourself in the pleasures of chocolate exploding in your taste buds, you will amazed at how satisfied you feel after eating a very small amount!

music and dance

Listen to music

The capacity of music to arouse powerful emotions and communicate states of consciousness, transmute feelings and ease inner tension has been recognised since time immemorial. More peak experiences are found to have been triggered by music than by sex or drugs. It is hardly surprising that nearly all religions make use of the inspirational effect of music to move and draw followers together, purify their souls and bring them closer to an experience of the divine.

Just as striking, and confirmed by research findings, is the ability of music to lower stress levels and reduce anxiety. Classical music has been found to have the most calming effect, and there is strong evidence that it boosts brain power – the so-called 'Mozart effect', but any kind of music you enjoy will do just as well.

Tuning in

If you feel emotionally wrought, play music that mirrors your mood, but follow up with something soothing and joyful. Personal taste affects what music you find relaxing, so turn to your own collection of CDs, tapes or albums and pick out your favourites, or try (excerpts from) the following classical music suggestions:

- Bach's *Air on a G String*, Suite No. 3
- Beethoven's *Spring Sonata* for violin, Op. 24; *Emperor Concerto* for piano No. 5, Op. 73; *Pathétique Sonata* for piano No. 8, Op. 13
- Mozart's *Eine Kleine Nachtmusik Serenade* No. 13
- Schubert's *Ave Maria* or *Impromptu* No. 3, Op. 142.

Alternatively there are tapes using natural sounds, such as those of dolphins, waves, birdsong and so on to relieve stress which are now widely available.

Make music

An excellent way to take time out is to learn a musical instrument. A brilliant stress reliever – the intellectual challenge involved takes your mind off every-thing else – and a lyrical means of expressing and transforming feelings and emotions. Ten minutes regular practice will lower your stress levels, stretch your mind and increase your appreciation of and response to other forms of music.

Dance to the music

Salsa, funk, hip-hop or a sedate waltz – dancing is fun, good for
your body and a great way to let off steam and relieve stress. You're
never too old to take to the floor, so don't be put off because you
don't know the moves. People dance in all sorts of ways and the rule
is that there are no rules – especially when you get do it in the privacy
of your own home.

   If you want to improve your technique, dance classes teaching
everything from ballet to jazz, from the samba to the cha-cha-cha,
abound. But for ten-minute stress relief all you need to boogie is
some lively music with a strong beat. Move to the rhythm and let
your instincts take over.

take up a hobby

There's more to life than slaving away in the office and coming home to domestic chores. The word 'hobby' may bring to mind nerds and anoraks, but there is enormous satisfaction and great stress relief to be had from doing something purely for pleasure, not to mention the numerous other benefits. Pursuing other interests is relaxing simply because it takes your mind off problems and anxieties. It also keeps your brain active, creates balance in your life, buffers you against blows such as the loss of a job or the breakdown of a relationship, makes you a more interesting human being and even, sometimes, becomes an alternative source of income.

Riding and fishing, painting and pottery may be out if you have only ten minutes, but there are plenty of creative pursuits on which you can spend ten minutes or several hours, depending on how long you have got.

Music, song and dance are time-honoured ways to express emotions and release tension. Games are another good way to de-stress at the end of the day. Set up a goal-post in your back garden and take pot-shots, or work out your frustrations with a punch bag. For something more intellectually challenging play chess, though this may take longer than ten minutes.

Gardening

Gardening is one of our national pastimes, and rightly so. Not only is it an enjoyable and creative way to spend time outdoors, which in itself lowers stress levels, but the end result is an outdoor sanctuary where you can sit and relax, and get away from it all. You do not need a large garden or green fingers, or to spend hours weeding, pruning and rotting compost, to create your very own stress-free zone. With a little planning you can construct a low maintenance garden which gives you time to just be in it and enjoy it.

As well as indulging your particular plant passions, consider adding a water feature. Water, especially flowing water, brings serenity and tranquillity: dig a pond and plant water lilies, build a fountain and relax to the gurgling of water, or install a birdbath. Investing in a meditative garden statue or sculpture – a seated Buddha or other image that symbolizes peace – will trigger calm thoughts. Bring music into your garden with the tinkling of wind chimes. And don't forget the most important thing – a comfortable garden seat for you to sit and relax in. Swinging in a hammock is a great way to unwind if you have got the space.

write it down

When you are under a lot of mental or emotional stress, writing down feelings, worries and anxieties is a safe way of letting off steam and getting things off your chest. Ten minutes spent putting pen to paper – or tapping away on your keyboard – helps you clarify your thoughts, get things in perspective and puts space between you and whatever or whomever you perceive as a problem.

An added bonus is that in the process of calming yourself down and giving vent to your feelings, you may find that writing helps you tap into your unconscious. You suddenly see things in a new light, and find solutions to problems. Nobody except you is going to see what you have written, so don't worry about style. Simply let whatever comes into your head spill out onto paper – it can be a stream of consciousness, or a series of headings. Keep a 'stress diary' or write a letter to whomever you see as the source of your problems. Best not send it, though…

de-clutter

The feng shui concept of de-cluttering has assumed the proportions of a religion, but the therapeutic benefits of a good clear-out and spring-clean are nothing new. Living and working knee-deep in chaos, stuff, junk, mess and disorder is stressful and unsettling. Clearing the clutter is enormously satisfying, liberating, curiously relaxing and truly cathartic. As you throw out the physical junk, the mental and emotional junk follows.

Spend ten minutes regularly clearing out clothes you never wear, books you will never open again, paperwork you don't need, gifts from well-meaning relatives you never liked in the first place but still hold on to, and so on. Target one area at a time – wardrobe, car, the coat cupboard, a kitchen drawer – and make a clean sweep. Decide what you want to keep, what can go to charity, what is garbage.

Clearing, cleaning and organising your external environment transforms it into a relaxing, healing place to be. By osmosis you simultaneously feel internally clearer and lighter. Stress levels fall, energy levels rise.

deep relaxation

This technique, based on yoga, completely relaxes the mind and body by a process of progressively releasing muscular tension in each and every part of the body. As you let go of physical tension, the mind automatically relaxes and becomes quiet. Relaxing in this way destroys fatigue and alleviates stress and stress-related symptoms such as headaches, migraine and insomnia. You may find it helpful to record the instructions below, leaving a sufficient pause in which to relax each body part before moving on to the next.

Instructions

1 Lie flat on your back in the corpse position (see p. 39).

2 Close your eyes and focus on your breathing. Take a few slow deep breaths, inhaling to a count of four, exhaling to a count of four, then allow your breath to settle into a light, even, relaxed rhythm.

3 Now turn your attention to releasing tension by consciously relaxing each part of the body in turn. First bring your attention to your feet for a few moments and send them the message to let go. Relax them as deeply as you can and then move your awareness on to your calves and repeat the process.

4 Work your way up the body in the same fashion, relaxing your thighs, buttocks, hips, abdomen, lower back, chest, upper back, hands, forearms, upper arms, shoulders, throat, neck and head.

5 Pay especial attention to the subtle art of relaxing your face. Relax your jaw and mouth, allowing your lips to part slightly and your tongue to rest in the lower half of your mouth. Relax your cheeks. Relax your eyes, allowing them to sink into the sockets. Relax your brows, forehead and temples. Feel your skin softening over your features as your facial muscles completely relax. Now relax your scalp and all the muscles in your head.

6 Scan your entire body from the tips of your toes to the top of your scalp. Breathe into any remaining pockets of tension. Let go and relax as you breathe out.

7 You are now completely relaxed. As the full weight of your body rests on the floor feel yourself sinking into the ground.

8 Once again become aware of your breathing and remain in the position for another five or ten minutes.

This technique may be combined with the method of rapid relaxation (see p. 106), which involves tensing and then letting go of the muscles in each part of the body. Always begin with rapid relaxation then continue with deep relaxation.

83

ten-minute cures

This section targets the tension hot-spots – eyes, head, neck, shoulders and back – and gives you remedies that really work to ease tension and soothe aches and pains. You may be surprised to find that the cures for headaches centre on releasing tension in other parts of the body, but in fact the most common cause of headaches is tension in the back of the neck.

Use the body check (see p. 102) to correct your posture, then pick and mix remedies according to your needs and the time available, or combine the cures with breathing exercises (see p. 101) and rapid relaxation (see pp. 106–7).

eye strain

Aching, strained eyes are often a symptom of stress, which causes the eyes to dry out, makes them prone to infection, and can lead to blurred vision, excessive sensitivity to light and other problems. Driving, reading, working at a screen, watching TV and fatigue can all cause or contribute to eye strain, which is aggravated by air conditioning, pollution, or strip lighting. To relieve eye strain:

- rest and relax your eyes by palming (see below)
- blink to moisten dry eyes
- take frequent breaks from the computer or when driving long distances
- splash your eyes (see p. 54)
- keep your eyes fit with regular eye exercises.

Just like any other muscles, the eye muscles need regular exercise to keep them strong and healthy. The eye exercises on page 66 will strengthen the muscles, relieve and help prevent eyestrain. They will also improve your sight if practised once or twice a day. Exercises to relieve headaches (see p. 87) and eye splashing (see p. 54) will also help relieve eye strain. Follow eye exercises with palming.

85

Palming
Palming relaxes and refreshes tired eyes, and can be done lying down or sitting with the elbows supported so that your back is straight and there is no pressure on your neck, shoulders or arms.

Instructions
1 Sit on a chair with your elbows supported at a height that allows you to cup your hands over your eyes keeping your back straight. Alternatively you can sit on the floor with your back supported by a wall, resting your elbows on your knees, or you can lie on the floor on your back with knees raised and feet flat on the floor.

2 Rub your hands together briskly, creating enough friction to warm the palms. Place your cupped hands over your closed eyes without touching them, so the outer edges of your palms make firm contact with your face and the fingers are crossed over your forehead and all light is excluded.

3 Hold your hands in place for five or ten minutes. Let the heat and dark soothe and relax your eyes. Become aware of your breathing. Feel your eyes becoming energised and invigorated as you breathe in, feel them relaxing as you breathe out tension.

Puffy eyes

For puffy eyes, drink a glass of hot water then lie back in the corpse pose (see p. 39) for ten minutes. The hot water helps to kick-start the kidneys and draw out retained water from the delicate tissue around the eyes. As you lie back, close your eyes and become aware of your breathing, without altering the natural flow of the breath. If your body feels tense, practice deep muscle relaxation (see p. 82).

Acupressure

Similar to massage, acupressure uses thumb and finger pressure at key points of the body to release tension and promote self-healing. Try the following, applying pressure for at least a minute:

● Breathing deeply, press firmly upwards with your thumbs into the indentations at the upper edges of the eye sockets closest to the bridge of your nose.

● Using your thumb, firmly press the 'third eye' point midway between the eyebrows, where the bridge of the nose meets the forehead.

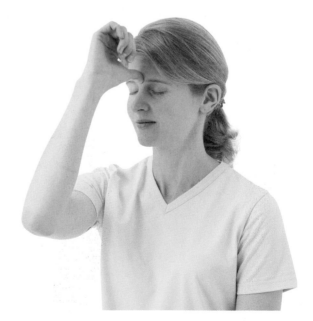

headaches, stiff necks and shoulders

There are many kinds and causes of headaches, but tight muscles around the head, especially those of the face, neck and scalp, caused by stress or poor posture, are the main cause of tension headaches. Mild or severe, they can last for days or even weeks, and while over-the-counter drugs help relieve pain they do nothing to relieve the tense muscles which are the root of the problem. However if you recognise the first signs of a headache and take early action you can often ease it, without recourse to tablets, simply by relaxing the muscles with gentle stretching and massage, or with acupressure, aromatherapy, hot baths, and deep relaxation.

▼ Cross-legged forward bend with head support

A relaxing position which helps ease stiffness in the neck and shoulders.

Instructions

1 Sit cross-legged on a firm cushion, folded blanket, or telephone directory with a support for your head in front. The head support could be the seat of a chair or sofa, or a pile of books, far enough away for you to be able to lengthen your back and rest your head comfortably on it.

2 Bend forward, resting your head on the support, adjusting your position or that of your support if necessary.

3 Let your head rest heavily. Close your eyes, part your teeth and soften your face. Stay in the position for 2–5 minutes.

Focus points
- Let your shoulders release. Feel them soften and broaden.
- Relax the back of your neck and abdomen.
- You should be comfortable in this position. Make any adjustments to your sitting position or head support as appropriate.

87

▼ Right-angle bend with head support

This position has a quietening effect on the mind. Resting your head in this way releases tension in the shoulders and neck, and the pressure on the forehead releases tension in the face, eyes and head.

Instructions

1 Place a folded blanket or a cushion on a table or kitchen worktop.

2 Stand facing the table with your feet hip width apart and your toes pointing forward, about a foot or more away.

3 Bend forward and clasp each elbow with the opposite hand. Extend your forearms away from your body and over your head if you can. Rest your forehead on your folded arms or, if your shoulders are not too stiff, directly on the table with your forearms extended beyond. Adjust the position of your feet so your legs are vertical and your back elongated.

◀ Legs up the wall

Opens the chest, relaxes shoulders, neck and head, and soothes tired feet. Also good for overall relaxation, especially when combined with awareness of your breathing. Avoid this position if you are menstruating.

Instructions

1 Place a thick cushion, bolster or folded blanket a few inches away from the wall and sit on it sideways to the wall, with your knees to your chest. Using your hands on the floor just behind you for support, take one leg followed by the other up the wall, lowering your back, shoulders, neck and head gently to the floor.

2 Adjust your position so that your buttocks and thighs are on or close to the wall, while your lower back is resting on the support.

3 Place your arms, palms up, on the floor to the sides of your support. Close your eyes and relax in the position, breathing slowly and evenly, for five minutes.

4 To come out of the position bend your knees, roll over to one side, then come up into a sitting position.

89

Other recommended exercises

- The Lion releases tension in the tongue, jaws, lips, throat and facial muscles (see p. 105).
- Bathroom Bends – Chest opener, Shoulder release and Right-angle bends to ease stiffness in the shoulders and upper back (see p. 54).
- De-stress at your desk – The workaholics workout
- Alternate nostril breathing (see p. 112).

Self-massage

Massaging your head, neck, forehead and temples not only feels good, but helps the muscles relax and encourages the flow of blood to the head. Try any of the following:

- Place your hands, outstretched, around the front, sides and top of your head and massage the head by rotating first your thumbs and fingertips in small circles so that the skin is moved over the scalp, then using the palms of your hands in a similar way.
- Using the fingertips as if you were washing your hair, massage the whole of the scalp using small circular movements.
- Run your fingernails like a comb through your hair from front to back, and from the top of your head down to the sides, in long, sweeping movements.

Aromatherapy

Particularly good oils for headaches are lavender and chamomile, both of which are calming as well as being natural painkillers, and peppermint, another very effective painkiller which helps relax the muscles. Use on their own or combine lavender with either peppermint or chamomile in equal quantities and:

- put a few drops on a handkerchief or tissue and inhale
- blend a couple of drops with a teaspoon of a carrier oil, such as almond or grapeseed, and rub into your temples
- add six to eight drops to a hot bath as you run the water in, and relax in a soothing aromatic bath for ten minutes.

90

Acupressure

Similar to massage, acupressure uses thumb and finger pressure at key points of the body to release tension and promote self-healing. Try the following, applying pressure for at least a minute, and preferably three:

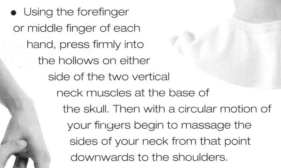

- Using the forefinger or middle finger of each hand, press firmly into the hollows on either side of the two vertical neck muscles at the base of the skull. Then with a circular motion of your fingers begin to massage the sides of your neck from that point downwards to the shoulders.

- Holding the thumb and index finger of the one hand fairly close together, press the flesh between them with the thumb and index finger of other hand, at the point just above the muscle.

- Using your thumb, firmly press the point midway between the eyebrows, where the bridge of the nose meets the forehead (see p. 86).

backaches

Chronic back pain is a leading cause of time off work and most people suffer from backache at some point in their lives. Stiffness in the lower spine caused by tension, a sedentary lifestyle, inactivity and poor posture, leads to back pain which can become persistent or lead to more serious problems if ignored.

Since immobility is a prime cause of back pain, resting in bed is not recommended. Fortunately most back pain can be cured – for good – through regular, controlled stretches and appropriate exercise, adopting good postural habits (see the Body Check, pp. 64 and 102), and taking regular short breaks throughout the day to prevent stress from building up. Always take action to ease back pain before it becomes severe with gentle stretching exercises, which are the only way to restore spinal mobility and flexibility and prevent further pain. For temporary relief from back pain apply heat to the affected part of the back, relax in a hot bath with essential oils, or try acupressure. The exercises below are based on yoga which, with its emphasis on spinal health, is excellent for both preventing and relieving back pain.

◄ **Knee squeezes**

Lying on your back and bringing your knees to your chest is one of the
fastest ways to ease tension, stiffness and pain in the back. The rocking
variation gently massages the spine and brings rapid relief for stiff backs.

Instructions

1 Lie on the floor with your knees bent and your feet flat on the ground,
close to your buttocks.

2 Breathe out and bring one knee to your chest, clasping your hands to your
knee or upper shin to hold it in place.

3 Hold for a few moments then release and repeat with the other leg.

4 Repeat twice on each side, then with both legs together.

5 *Variation*: If your back pain is not too severe, breathe in and bring both
knees to your chest as before, then raise your chin to your knees. Lower
your head back to the floor and then gently rock from side to side, and then
in a circular movement, first in one direction then the other.

6 Breathe out and return to the starting position for a few moments.

7 Turn to one side and sit up carefully.

Focus points
● To protect the vertebrae place a thick blanket beneath you before rocking.
● Keep rocking movements steady, controlled and rhythmic.

93

▶ Kneeling forward bend

This relaxing position stretches your spine and helps keep
it flexible.

Instructions

1 Start in the Kneeling position (see p. 38), using a cushion
beneath your buttocks if required.

2 If back pain is severe, place a folded blanket or thick towel
across your thighs, tucking it underneath your abdomen.

3 Place your hands in front and bend forward slowly,
resting your forehead on the floor.

4 Hold for a minute or two, or as long as you
feel comfortable.

94

Focus points

● Rest your head on a cushion or other
support if it does not reach the floor.
● Once back pain has eased,
continue to practice the posture as
a preventative measure to keep
your spine healthy, omitting the
towel across your lap.

▼ Cross-legged forward bend

This pose combines a supported forward bend with a gentle spinal twist, which eases and prevents backache and increases the elasticity of the spine.

Instructions

1 Sit on a cushion or other support on the floor with your legs crossed at the shins, not the ankles, and with the right leg in front.

2 Turn your body to the right and bend over your right leg, holding the position for 30–60 seconds.

3 Change the cross of the legs and repeat on the other side.

Focus points

● If your head does not reach the floor use a support such as a chair or a pile of books to rest it.
● When bending to one side, keep the opposite hip down so the buttock remains on the floor.

95

▼ Chair rest

This position relaxes the back and takes the pressure off the lower back.

Instructions

1 Lie on one side at right angles to a stool, chair or sofa, with your knees towards your chest.

2 Turn onto your back and place your calves on the chair and relax for five or ten minutes.

3 Bring your legs towards your chest, turn to the side and sit up carefully.

Focus point

● Placing a weight on your abdomen – a heavy cushion or book, or a large bag of rice or sugar, helps release the lower back.

◀ Squatting

A quarter of the human race still squat rather sit in sit on high-backed chairs, and by doing so keep their backs strong, flexible and relaxed. Frequent squatting is one of the best possible ways to keep your spine healthy and prevents back problems. It also strengthens legs, ankles and feet, and keeps hips and knees flexible.

Caution

Do not squat while you are suffering severe back pain or if you have bad knee problems. Begin practising once you are over the worst of it to insure against further problems. Do not stay in the squatting position for any length of time if you have varicose veins.

Instructions

1 Stand with your feet parallel and slightly apart, resting your heels on a thick book or telephone directory if necessary.

2 Lower yourself down so that you are sitting on your heels.

3 Spread your knees a little way apart and rest your elbows on them, clasping your hands together. Hold the position for a minute or two, or as long as you comfortably can.

Focus points

● If you need support as you go down, hold the back of a heavy chair or table.
● If you have knee problems, go down only so far as feels comfortable. If in doubt, don't do it.

Other recommended exercises

- Bathroom bends – Right-angle bend, turning the toes inwards (p. 54)
- Workaholic's workout – Unwind your spine, Ease your back, using a thick towel or folded blanket across the thighs and tucking it underneath the abdomen (pp. 68 and 94)

Heat and aromatherapy treatments

Heat soothes and loosens tight muscles, easing painful backs. One of the most relaxing ways to apply heat is simply to soak in a warm bath for ten minutes with a few drops of lavender, eucalyptus, rosemary or ginger, all of which ease muscular aches and pains, or with other relaxing essential oils of your choice (see p. 112).

Alternatively – or afterwards – lie down on your tummy on the floor, or on a very firm mattress, in a warm room free from draughts. Place a folded blanket under your abdomen to support and slightly lift your back, then rest your head on your arms and place a hot water bottle wrapped in a towel on the painful area. To enhance relaxation rub a few drops of essential oils (see above) mixed with a carrier oil such as almond into the affected part of your back before placing the hot water bottle. Relax in this position for ten minutes.

Acupressure

Acupressure, which uses thumb and finger pressure at key points of the body to release tension and promote self-healing, is another effective way to release muscular tension in the lower back.

● Sitting on a chair or lying on your back on the floor, with your knees bent and feet flat on the floor, place your fingertips at the point two finger widths below your belly button and press firmly into the abdomen for a minute.

● Lying on your back on the floor, with your knees and feet raised so your lower legs are at right angles to the floor, place your fingertips in the centre of the crease at the back of the knee and press firmly for a minute. As you do so rock your legs backwards and forwards with your arms to increase the pressure.

quick fixes

Ten minutes is a long time if you find yourself suddenly thrown into a confrontation, or any other threatening or upsetting situation. But unless you are in immediate physical danger, avoid acting on impulse and instead take refuge in a quick fix. Although they are not a substitute for regular exercise and mental relaxation, these instant stress-busters can make all the difference between keeping a grip and completely losing it.

Most of these rapid relaxation techniques can be used wherever you happen to be – at work, in the car, at the dinner table – whenever you need a quick stress-busting fix. Make time to work off stress and completely relax as soon as you can.

take a **deep breath**

Deep breathing is the best and quickest stress buster in the universe, and the great thing is that you really can do it any time, any place!

For rapid and effective emergency stress relief try any of the following breathing techniques, sitting or standing with your shoulders relaxed and your back comfortably upright. Breathe through your nose, not your mouth, throughout all the techniques and if you have already learned the techniques of abdominal or complete breathing (see p. 113 and p. 121), then breathe from the abdomen to maximize stress relief.

- Focus on your breathing and take in a slow, deep breath to a slow count of four (seconds), then exhale slowly to a count of eight. Repeat two or three times, then take a few normal breaths, then repeat the slow deep breaths.
- Breathe in slowly and deeply to a slow count of four (seconds), hold for four seconds without strain, then breathe out to a count of four. Repeat a few times.
- Close your eyes if possible, then take two or three deep breaths. With each exhalation feel that you are releasing any tension, with each inhalation feel yourself refreshed and energized.
- Focusing on your solar plexus (between the navel and the breastbone), become aware of your breath as it flows in and out, noting the rise and fall of your abdomen. Tell yourself 'All is well. I feel calm.'

101

spritz away stress

Banish stress instantly with a quick spritz of soothing essential oils. There are some excellent products – creams and gels as well as sprays – available on the market or you can buy an atomizer and create your own blend. Lavender is a versatile oil which relieves most symptoms of stress and combines well with others. Try it with sandalwood and rose, or sandalwood and geranium, for instant relaxation. Other oils for specific symptoms include:

- Headaches   basil, eucalyptus, peppermint
- Migraine   chamomile, peppermint
- Muscle tension   chamomile, clary sage, rosemary
- Anger   neroli, rosewood, sandalwood
- Anxiety   clary sage, melissa, neroli, rosewood, patchouli
- Burnout   bergamot, rosemary

Carry your favourite oil or blend around in your bag or pocket and spritz temples, earlobes or the insides of your wrists. Combine with gentle massage of the temples, or the back of the neck, for extra relief. Alternatively put a couple of drops of your chosen fragrance or combination onto a handkerchief and take a deep inhalation whenever you need a quick pick-me-up or instant stress-buster.

carry your favourite oil or blend around in your bag and spritz temples, earlobes or the insides of your wrists

smile, laugh, roar

Simply by altering your facial expression or having a laugh (even a forced laugh) you can you can lift your mood and let go of tension and negativity in a matter of moments. If you are too stressed to smile or a laugh, then roar.

Grin like a Cheshire cat

It is impossible to feel miserable or stressed with a broad smile on your face. If you cannot manage a genuine smile of enjoyment, then fake it – it often leads to the real thing. Smiling, even when simulated, immediately alters your frame of mind, making you feel instantly better about yourself. The knock-on effect is that people then respond to you much more positively.

Laugh like a hyena

A good belly laugh not only gives you a natural high (stimulating the production of endorphins), it is great way to relax and relieve stress. Along with an array of health benefits, laughter exercises and releases tension in the muscles of the face, scalp, neck, torso, shoulders, arms and legs, and suppresses the production of stress hormones. And it keeps you looking and feeling young!

You don't need an endless repertoire of funny jokes or to be brilliantly witty – all you need is the ability to see the funny side of life – and stressful situations. As with smiling, if you cannot come up with genuine belly laughter, then fake it till you make it. Laughter – even fake laughter – is infectious.

Roar like a lion

Because it involves making a pretty grotesque facial expression, not to mention sticking your tongue out, it takes courage to do this in public. That said, the Lion pose is a great stress-buster which strengthens, tones and eases tension in the tongue, jaws, lips, throat and facial muscles. In addition to relieving stress, regular practice of the pose tightens the facial muscles, improving appearance, and is said to improve the voice quality and to prevent or cure sore throats.

Sit in the kneeling position (see p. 38) with your hands palms down on your knees. Take a deep inhalation then exhale forcefully until your lungs are empty, making an *aaargh* sound as you do so. At the same time open your eyes and mouth as wide as possible, stretch your tongue out as far as it will go, as though silently roaring, straighten your arms, stretch out your fingertips, and tense the whole body. Hold for as long as you can, then close your mouth and breathe in through your nose. Take a few normal breaths then repeat.

Although traditionally performed in the kneeling position, as a quick stress-buster you can do the Lion in any comfortable position – at your desk or in the driving seat of your car.

rapid **relaxation 1**

A few brief minutes is not long enough for deep relaxation, but rapid relaxation can be effectively achieved by first tensing then letting go of groups of muscles. The instructions given below are for rapid relaxation in the corpse position (lying on the floor), but the method can easily be adapted for sitting in a chair or standing up.

Instructions

1 Lie flat on your back in the corpse position (see p. 39).

2 Take a deep abdominal breath and raise the legs and feet a few inches above the floor, stiffening them as you do so. Hold them tense for five or six seconds then simultaneously breathe out and let go of your legs, allowing them to drop to the floor.

3 Now, in a similar way, breathe in and lift your buttocks, tensing and clenching the muscles together, then breathe out and let go. Carry on with the arms and hands, making a fist with your arms, then your upper body.

4 Finally breathe in and, without lifting your head, open your eyes and mouth as wide as you can and stick out your tongue as in the Lion (see p. 105). Breathe out and relax. Then breathe in and screw your face up in the reverse of the Lion expression. Breathe out and relax.

5 Lie flat on the floor in the original position for a few moments and completely relax. Feel that your body is very heavy, so heavy that it is sinking into the floor.

6 To come out of the relaxation bend your knees so your feet are flat on the floor, roll over to one side, then push yourself up using the other arm.

rapid relaxation 2

For even quicker relaxation, instead of tensing and relaxing groups of muscles, lie in the corpse position as previously, then breathe in and raise the legs, upper body and arms all at the same time a few inches from the floor. Hold the whole body tense for five or six seconds, then breathe out, let go and relax as before.

If you are unable to lie down, you can still use the technique of tightening and then relaxing all the muscles to release physical tension in almost any position.

switch off

Instead of relaxing after work, many people spend much of their free time thinking about work issues and problems. If the result is constructive solutions and fresh ideas, great, but paradoxically if you can switch off and relax you are more likely to be a creative and effective problem solver.

If the stress of work dominates your private life, establish rituals to help you disconnect from work and usher in your free time. A large G&T is a time-honoured custom, and very effective too, but remember that stress can lead to reliance on alcohol and there are other, healthier options.

To help you mentally clock off and detach from the business of the day spend ten minutes before leaving work or when you get home reviewing the day and planning the

from work

next. If there are issues you cannot discuss or resolve at work then spend ten or twenty minutes talking it over with a partner or friend. Then leave work behind you and relax.

If you have spent most of the day sitting, go out for a run or do some exercises at home. Although sun salutations (page 48) are traditionally performed in the morning, they are an excellent way to get moving any time of day. After a hard day one of the most relaxing things you can do is soak in a warm bath when you get home. This is also a good time for calming breathing exercises and meditation, but if that sounds too much like more hard work (it isn't!), at least try to devote ten minutes just to yourself, sitting out in the garden, taking a stroll, listening to music, reading a book, and enjoying yourself.

plan your day

People who use their time wisely and efficiently not only fit a lot more into twenty-four hours than the rest of us, but save themselves a lot of unnecessary stress. Being busy does not have to mean being stressed, and by managing your time well you can still make time for relaxation and fun as well as work.

To make time you need to spend time. Set aside ten minutes each day to review the day, and to plan and prioritize for the following day. If you cannot find time for this before leaving work, or when you get back home after work, then make time in the morning, or use time spent travelling to think and plan.

- Make a 'to do' list, and note down all the tasks, projects and goals you need/want to accomplish. Include a balance of leisure, relaxation and physical exercise as well as work activities, and a wish list – things you would like to do if you have time.
- Go through your list and, using a highlighter pen or coding system (for example A-1, A-2, A-3…), mark out all the urgent and high-priority tasks that must be done today. Then, using a different colour or coding system (B-1, B-2…), go through marking the medium-priority tasks that are less urgent, but must still be done in the next few days. With a third colour or code (C-1, C-2…), mark the low-priority tasks that are less urgent but still important.
- Starting with the top priorities, assess approximately how much time you will need to spend on each task.
- Plan the day, and if possible timetable any time-consuming or demanding tasks and projects for early in the day, when you will be fresh and full of energy, and leave small or routine tasks for later. You work better when you are refreshed and relaxed, so remember to build in regular breaks and breathers – for exercise, meditation and ten-minute stress-busters.
- Allocate time for routine tasks – post, emails, phone messages, and so on – rather than constantly checking for messages. Three times a day is generally sufficient.
- Allow some time – at least 10 per cent of your day – to accommodate unforeseen and unexpected tasks.

Once you have completed your list you can use the following affirmations, or others of your own creating, as positive reinforcement:

- *I achieve my goals/accomplish my tasks calmly and quickly.*
- *I am organised and I manage my time effectively.*
- *I enjoy the challenge of getting things done.*

During the day add to the list as new tasks come up and tick off those now done. Be ruthless about getting through the most important tasks. At the end of the day or next morning, when planning the forthcoming day, review and renew your list.

Are you satisfied with your use of time?

High-priority tasks

If high-priority items are not being accomplished, ask yourself why.
● Are you creating for yourself or being given an unrealistic workload? If so are there any tasks you can delegate? Can you discuss your workload with your boss or supervisor?
● Are you being constantly interrupted by inessential phone calls or people stopping by to chat or ask advice? If so establish boundaries, making it clear when you are available and when you are off limits and should not be interrupted – either because you need to concentrate on important tasks, or because you are taking time out for yourself. Put the phone on automatic answering mode.

Tasks that keep reappearing on your to-do list
● If the same medium- or low-priority task appears on the list day after day, week after week, without moving up or down the list, either delegate it, do it, strike it off your list, or timetable it in your diary for a later, but immovable except for emergencies, time.
● If a high- or medium-priority task is not getting done, ask yourself why. Are you putting off making a decision? If you have all the facts at your fingertips don't put off making decisions. Unresolved problems build tension and dissipate energy.

Me-time
● Have you accomplished any of the items on your wish list? Aim to tick off at least one wish-list item, no matter how small, a day. Last but not least, have you taken regular 10-minute breaks to keep your stress levels in control?

relax in an aromatic bath

There's nothing better than a warm, fragrant bath for soothing frazzled nerves and tired bodies after a stressful day. Make sure your bathroom is cosy and warm, switch off or dim the lights, or use candles, then add essential oils (see below) or Epsom salts to your bath water and lie back and relax. Listen to your favourite music or enjoy the silence, closing your eyes and feeling the warmth of the water washing over you. Visualize your worries being washed away.

Essential oils that help you unwind and relax include bergamot, chamomile, clary sage, geranium, lavender, lemon, marjoram, neroli, patchouli, rose, sandalwood and ylang-ylang. For an aromatic bath add six to eight drops to your bath as you run the water, swishing it around well before you get in. Bergamot, geranium, lavender, rose and sandalwood are all very fragrant oils which can be used on their own for a relaxing bath time experience or in combination with other oils.

Let your own nose guide you when blending oils, but as a rough guide good combinations include lavender or lemon with almost anything, but especially good for stress is lavender combined with chamomile, geranium, rose, sandalwood or ylang-ylang. Alternatively, for something a little more exotic, try the combination of patchouli and ylang-ylang. When using a mix of two oils use four drops of each in your bath water.

For a relaxing and fragrant combination of three oils try three drops each of rose, ylang-ylang and sandalwood; rose, lavender and sandalwood; or chamomile, sandalwood and ylang-ylang.

After your bath, add the same blend of oils to some body lotion and massage it into your skin working from your feet upwards.

breathe **deeply**

Abdominal breathing

Animals and babies instinctively breathe correctly – taking deep, relaxed breaths, as you can see from the way their abdomens rise and fall with each breath. But with the passing of the years we tend to develop faulty breathing habits, using only the upper part of the chest. Stress is particularly associated with shallow breathing, which in its turn leads to more tension and anxiety, creating a vicious circle. Unless this kind of breathing is replaced by deep diaphragmatic breathing, using the abdominal muscles, it is almost impossible to relax, mentally or physically.

Practising the technique of abdominal breathing helps to correct shallow breathing by encouraging movement of the diaphragm and abdomen, allowing the lungs to fill to capacity and expel air more efficiently.

Instructions

Stretch out on your back in the corpse position (see p. 39). Close your eyes and breathe in slowly and evenly through your nostrils. Feel your abdomen swelling and rising, then your ribcage expanding and finally your upper chest filling with air. Pause briefly before breathing out fully. As you release the breath note the reverse movement. Feel your abdomen falling, the ribcage contracting, and finally the upper chest lowering as the air is expelled. Pause briefly before breathing in again. Repeat this cycle in a flowing, steady movement for a few minutes and then let your breathing return to normal. A relaxing variation is to breathe in to a count of four, and out to a count of eight, for six to twelve complete breaths before letting your breathing return to normal.

To establish the habit of breathing deeply and healthily, focus your attention several times a day on your breathing – you can be lying down, sitting up, standing or walking around – and consciously breathe from the abdomen for a minute or two.

Bellows breathing

Bellows breathing, or *bhastrika*, is a powerful yogic breathing technique used to still the mind in preparation for meditation. It is also said to purify the body, improve digestion, help with the elimination of waste products and strengthen the abdominal muscles. Above all it is highly regarded by yogis as a potent way to arouse latent spiritual forces.

In this technique the breath is controlled entirely by rapid movements of the abdominal muscles, so it is best to master the technique of abdominal breathing (see p. 113) before attempting it. If you practise bellows breathing incorrectly, using your stomach instead of your abdominal muscles, you are liable to experience dizziness or nausea. Because bellows breathing is an intense and very vigorous technique, it is not suitable for people with heart, lung, eye or ear problems, with high or low blood pressure, or for pregnant women. If you have any doubts, take advice from your doctor or an experienced teacher before practising.

Bellows breathing is best practised on an empty stomach in an airy environment. Wait at least two hours after a light meal, five or six after a heavy one, before doing it and then another half-hour afterwards before eating again.

Instructions

Sit or kneel with your back straight in any of the meditation positions (see p. 36), except for the corpse pose, head and neck in line with the base of the spine, hands on knees. Begin breathing in and out rapidly through the nose by contracting the abdominal muscles quickly and forcibly, then immediately relaxing them again so that air is automatically drawn back into the lungs. Continue rhythmically for 10 breaths, gradually increasing to about 20. On the final exhalation contract the abdomen fully and empty the lungs completely. Take in a slow, deep, abdominal breath, and hold it as long as you comfortably can. Exhale completely to finish.

This completes one round of bellows breathing. Repeat two or three times, resting between rounds with a few normal breaths.

Lie in the corpse position (see p. 39) for a few minutes until your breathing has become quiet and still or sit for meditation.

114

mantra **meditation**

Just as you need to exercise regularly to keep fit, you need to establish a routine to reap the full benefits of meditation, ideally practising twice a day. Research shows that as well as gaining instant stress relief from meditation, regular meditators cope significantly better than others with the pressures of everyday life.

Silent repetition of a mantra is the most popular form of meditation. A mantra is a sacred or mystical sound, syllable or word thought to possess spiritual potency that affects the consciousness of the person who repeats it. The most famous of all mantras is the sacred syllable *om* (composed of the three sounds *a-u-m*), said to be the primordial sound from which the entire universe arises. Other mantras are often preceded by *om*, such as *om mani padme hum*, 'om, the jewel in the lotus', much used by Tibetan Buddhists, and *om namah shivaya*, a traditional Indian mantra honouring Shiva.

For the purposes of deep relaxation, however, a meaningless word or sound will do just as well. Choose any word or sound that appeals to you, the shorter the better, or use a positive word, phrase or affirmation, or even your own name. Once you have found a mantra you are comfortable with, stick to it and use it at odd moments during the day to relax you.

115

How to meditate using a mantra

In a quiet and peaceful room or corner, sit upright in a simple cross-legged position or in any of the meditation positions illustrated on page 36. Close your eyes and, breathing naturally, mentally repeat your chosen mantra in rhythm with your breathing, once or twice as you breathe in, once or twice as you breathe out. Focus your attention on the mantra and become absorbed in it. Whatever thoughts and feelings arise, just observe them passively. Let them be without engaging with them and gently bring your attention back to your mantra.

● Of all mantras, the most celebrated is the sacred syllable *om*. Its symbolic representation, shown here, is often used as a focus of visual meditation (see p. 124).

wind down

Towards the end of the day your body naturally starts to wind down. Energy levels drop and metabolism slows down.

Sleep is the greatest stress buster on the planet, so give yourself all the help you can to get a good night's kip. Avoid large meals close to bedtime, as they can interfere with sleep, weighing heavily on the stomach and causing indigestion. If possible have dinner at least two hours before bed.

If worrying about work problems keeps you awake, make a list of things to do for the following day (see p. 110) and ensure that you give yourself time to detach from the business of the day before turning in.

gently

Help prepare yourself for sleep by devoting ten minutes to deep relaxation exercises, having a warm bath, listening to soothing music, doing some calming breathing exercises, meditation, reading a book or a combination of these. If sleep regularly eludes you, follow the tips for a better nights sleep on page 31.

Once you have turned down the light and lain down to sleep, close your eyes and stretch out on your back. Become aware of your breathing, and without trying to alter the natural flow, simply watch it as it enters and leaves your body while you drift into deep, refreshing sleep.

on your back

Most exercises have both a calming and an energizing effect, which can lead to broken nights if done too close to bedtime. The following exercises, however, will help to release and unwind you, especially after a warm bath, without affecting your sleep.

All the movements should be done slowly and softly, as if moving through syrup. Breathe evenly and rhythmically throughout, focusing on the exhalations, which should be long and slow. Use a small cushion beneath your head for extra comfort.

Instructions

1 Lay on your back, breathe in and bring your right knee to your chest, holding the shin with both hands. Breathe out and bring your leg closer. Breathe in and, as you breathe out, straighten the right leg back onto the floor. Repeat with the left leg. Repeat on both sides once more.

2 Hold both your shins just below your knees, bringing both knees to your chest. Rock slowly and gently from side to side, massaging your lower back on the floor, for about thirty seconds. Keeping them together, make small circles with your knees, first in a clockwise direction, then anti-clockwise (see pp. 92–93 for illustrations).

3 Now place your hands on your knees and push them away from you and then out. Make circles with your knees bringing them back into your chest. Continue for two more circles then reverse direction for another three, finishing with your knees in to your chest.

4 Keeping your knees to your chest, take your arms out sideways onto the floor a little lower than your shoulders, with your palms facing up. Breathe in and then lower your legs towards your left elbow as you breathe out, trying to keep your right shoulder on the floor. Let your left leg rest on the floor and relax your right leg towards your left leg, placing the cushion between your thighs if the legs do not come together. Stay for a couple breaths, relaxing a little further with each long exhalation. Breathe in and come back to the centre. Repeat to the right.

119

5 With your knees bent and your feet on the floor, and your arms out sideways as in the previous exercise, breathe in slowly, lifting the arms up to vertical. Move slowly as if pushing the air. Breathe out, lowering your arms over your head slowly towards the floor, keeping them straight but not overstretching. Breathe in and return to vertical. Breathe out and return your arms to the starting position. Repeat four to five times.

If you can, follow this sequence by relaxing in the corpse position (see p. 39).

complete breathing

In complete breathing you make full use of your lungs, though never to the point of strain or discomfort. This is a yogic technique similar to abdominal breathing (see p. 113), but instead of lying on your back you sit upright, which allows more air to be drawn in and produces a fuller sensation.

Complete breathing calms and steadies the mind, and energizes the whole system. It also relieves anxiety, lifts depression, and promotes clear and positive thinking. Once the technique has been mastered, it can be used at will in any circumstances for instant stress relief.

Instructions

1 Sit or kneel in any of the meditation positions on pages 36 to 38, keeping the back straight and the base of your spine, back of your neck and the top of your head in a line. Breathe in and out through your nostrils throughout. Now visualize your lungs as having three spaces – lower, middle and upper – and inhalation as happening in the three stages that follow.

2 As you begin to draw in air, the diaphragm pushes downwards into the abdomen, causing it to swell out as the lower space is filled.

3 As you continue to inhale, the ribcage expands as air is drawn into the middle space.

4 As you complete the inhalation, the upper chest broadens (but note that the shoulders are not lifted), as the upper space is filled with air.

Although the inhalation is visualized as happening in three stages, it should be a smooth, continuous movement. When your lungs feel comfortably full, hold the breath for a few seconds, then exhale in a smooth continuous movement. As you exhale, the air leaves the lower lungs first, then the middle, and then the upper lungs. If it feels comfortable to do so, you may pause for a few seconds before breathing in again.

Once you have grasped the movement, practise in an even, rhythmic fashion. To begin with keep to a ratio between inhalation, retention and exhalation of 1:1:1, to a count of about 4 for each inhalation. Then move on to a ration of 1:1:2, so if you inhale and hold to a count of 4, you then exhale to a count of 8.

Make four or five complete in-and-out breaths (taking about a minute), then breathe normally (abdominally) for half a minute, then do four or five more complete breaths. As you inhale, visualize yourself breathing in energy. As you exhale, visualize yourself breathing out tension and fatigue. Follow with alternate nostril breathing and/or meditation.

alternate nostril breathing

Once you have learnt the technique of complete breathing, you can go on to practice alternate nostril breathing, in which you breathe in through one nostril, retain the breath, then breathe out through the other nostril. This is another yogic method of breath control that has a very calming, relaxing effect and is especially helpful for people who suffer from insomnia.

Instructions

Sit or kneel in any of the meditation positions on pages 36 to 38, keeping the back straight and the base of your spine, back of your neck and the top of your head in a line. Blow each nostril in turn before you begin to clear it. Don't worry if one or other nostril is slightly blocked – it will probably clear during the exercise – but if either nostril is badly blocked use it for exhaling only to start with. Breathe smoothly and slowly, using the abdomen, throughout, and keep your facial muscles relaxed. Breathing rhythm is important in this exercise, the traditional ratio between inhalation, retention and exhalation being 1:4:2, here given as as count of 4, 16 and 8 respectively. However to avoid strain beginners are advised to keep to a ratio of 1:2:2, 1:1:2 or 1:1:1.

1 (In this breathing technique the right hand is traditionally used to open and close the nostrils, but if you are left-handed you may prefer to use your left hand.) Fold the index and middle fingers of your right hand into your palm and lift the hand up to your nose. Place your left hand palm upwards on your left knee or in your lap. Close your eyes.

2 Close your right nostril with your thumb and exhale through your left nostril until your lungs feel empty. Keeping your right nostril closed inhale fully to a count of 4, progressively filling your lower, middle and upper lungs.

3 Still keeping your right nostril blocked, close your left nostril with your ring and little fingers, so that both nostrils are blocked. Hold your breath to a count of 16. (If you are new to this exercise, or if it is uncomfortable, hold for a count of 8 or 4.)

4 Keeping your left nostril closed, release your thumb and breathe out through your right nostril to a count of 8. (If you are new to this exercise, or if it is uncomfortable, breathe out to a count of 4.) Still keeping your left nostril closed inhale fully to a count of 4, progressively filling your lower, middle and upper lungs.

123

5 Keeping your left nostril blocked, close your right nostril with your thumb, so that both nostrils are blocked. Hold your breath to a count of 16. (If you are new to this exercise or it is uncomfortable, hold for a count of 8 or 4.)

6 Keeping your right nostril closed, release your ring and little fingers and breathe out through your left nostril to a count of 8. (If you are new to this exercise, or if it is uncomfortable, breathe out to a count of 4.)

This completes one round. Start with two or three rounds and build up to six or more. As you breathe, focus your attention on the space in between your eyebrows.

Follow with a few minutes meditation – either breath awareness (p. 113), mantra meditation (p. 115) or visual meditation (p. 117).

visual meditation

This kind of meditation involves gazing steadily at an object such as a lighted candle, a flower, stone, ornament or piece of fruit. If you are spiritually or mystically inclined you may prefer to use a religious symbol such as the Christian cross, the yin-yang symbol or a yantra, the visual equivalent of a mantra (see p. 115). When your eyes tire you close them and visualize your chosen object with your mind's eye. A lighted candle in a darkened room is a popular choice because the eyes are naturally drawn to the brightness of the flame and the image is easy to retain when the eyes are closed.

How to meditate using a visual image

- In a quiet and peaceful room or corner, sit upright in a simple cross-legged position or in any of the meditation positions illustrated on page 36, having placed your chosen object about three to five feet away from you and roughly level with your eyes.
- Breathing naturally, focus your attention on the object and gaze at it in a steady, relaxed way, without staring, and blinking as usual whenever you need to. As soon as your eyes begin to tire close them and form a mental image of the object.
- If you become aware that you have lost concentration, or that your attention has wandered, gently bring it back to your meditation focus, and if necessary repeat the process of looking then forming a mental image.

- The Shri Yantra is one of the most celebrated of all mandalas. It represents the yogic vision of the cosmos and the evolutionary process, and is often used in meditation to draw the yoga practitioner inwards.

golden rules for keeping calm

1   Don't rush eating, speaking or moving

2   Eat and sleep well

3   Maintain good posture

4   Take regular exercise

5   Breathe deeply

6   Live in the present moment

7   Think positively; count blessings, not misfortunes

8   Replace negative self-talk with positive statements

9   Be more assertive

10 Observe good manners

11 Treat yourself and others with love and respect

12 Talk calmly and listen more attentively

13 Simplify and slow down the pace of your life

14 Keep your life in balance and make time for fun

15 Spend time outdoors

16 Accept responsibility for your life; don't blame others

17 Learn to recognise your own stress signals

18 Keep a sense of humour and have a laugh

19 Smile – fake it if need be

20 Take regular ten-minute breaks throughout the day

index

127

acknowledgements

I am grateful to Peggy Vance, who first suggested I write this book, and was always there to support and advise. I would also like to thank my editor Steve Guise for his tireless efforts and patience, and for providing much appreciated continuity throughout. Many thanks to Sandi Sharkey for modelling so beautifully and serenely, and to Paul Bricknell for his expertise behind the lens.

I am particularly indebted to Jo Robertson, one of the most gifted yoga teachers I have had the good fortune to be taught by, for devising most of the exercise sequences. Many thanks for your enthusiasm, experience, and above all for being such fun.

My love as always to Nick and Sam, and thanks for your warmth and humour. You have contributed enormously to my understanding of stress – and how to relieve it!